THE
'FLYING SCOTSMAN'
POCKET-BOOK

Introduction by R.H.N. Hardy

CONWAY

A Conway Book
© Conway, 2013
First published in Great Britain in 2013 by Conway, an imprint of
Anova Books Company Ltd
10 Southcombe Street
London W14 0RA
www.conwaypublishing.com
Twitter: @conwaybooks

Distributed in US and Canada by:
Sterling Publishing Co., Inc
387 Park Avenue South
New York, NY 10016–8810

10 9 8 7 6 5 4 3 2 1

Produced for Conway Books by Posthouse Publishing

To receive regular email updates on forthcoming Conway titles, email
conway@anovabooks.com with 'Conway Update' in the subject field.

British Library Cataloguing in Publication Data
A CIP catalogue for this book is available on request from the British Library

ISBN 9781844862221

Printed and bound by 1010 International Ltd, China

Picture acknowledgements

© Science and Society Picture Library, Pages 23, 25, 32, 43, 47, 49, 51, 53, 60, 84, 127
and for images contained in the colour section. © Mortons Ltd, 14, 15, 27, 29 top, 94,
96, 97 112, 120, 121. © Nick Boderick, 5. © Corbis Images, 7, 35, 66, 67 and for images
contained in colour section. © Brian Trenerry, 10. © Getty Images, 29 bottom, 38, 39,
79, 108, 122, 123. © Paul Bickerdyke, 128. © Les Nixon, 117. © Peter Marriott, 111. ©
Peter Lomas/Associated Newspapers/Rex Features, 83. The extract from *Railways in the
Blood* by R.H.N. Hardy reproduced with kind permission Ian Allan Publishing Ltd. The
illustrations on pages 74. 75, 76 are reproduced from *Famous Train Journeys No 1, Flying
Scotsman* by Alan Anderson.

CONTENTS

Captions to colour sections

First colour section: Page 1: The 'Then and Now' series of posters were produced for L.N.E.R., showing illustrations of both the first Flying Scotsman in 1862, and its modern equivalent in 1930. Page 2: Poster showing the stations and mileage on the Flying Scotsman route. Page 3: L.N.E.R. poster produced to promote the Flying Scotsman non-stop service. Page 4: The 'Then and Now' series of posters for L.N.E.R. to promote the 200 restaurant cars on the company's trains.

Second colour section: Page 1: The nameplate and driving wheel of the 'Flying Scotsman'.
Page 2 Top: 'Flying Scotsman' hauling the Cumbrian Mountain Express approaching Wennington Railway Station, 5 July, 1986. Bottom: 'Flying Scotsman', in its original apple-green livery of the L.N.E.R. hauls an excursion train out of Kings Cross Station in 1969. Page 3: 'Flying Scotsman', on its way to Skipton in West Yorkshire. Page 4: Clockwise from top left: Examples of luggage labels. 'Flying Scotsman' commemorative first day cover to celebrate visiting Australia in 1988. 'Flying Scotsman' menu. 'Flying Scotsman', departing York station in 2004. Wine list created on the centenary of the 'Flying Scotsman' service 1862–1962.

Introduction by R.H.N. Hardy

R.H.N. Hardy in the cab of 'Oliver Cromwell' at Norwich station in July 2011.

When this book was taking shape and I was asked to write the introduction, I wondered what on earth of interest could still be written about this famous locomotive and the express train so often hauled by its namesake. But once the draft had been compiled and I had read the opening pages, I realised how interesting and enjoyable it was to read in book form what I had first devoured as a teenager or even younger. Maybe my introduction should cover every article but this is not easy in the space allowed. However I shall do my best and also introduce a thought or two of my own, maybe of interest, maybe amusing, so we shall see.

Look at the three Pacific locomotives on pages 14 and 15. One was completely rebuilt in 1924, one lasted until 1937, very powerful but one might say rather difficult and the third was the fore-runner of a class of 'World Beaters'. That, of course was 1470, later to be named 'Great Northern' and was a London and North Eastern Railway (L.N.E.R.) class A1. A good engine, extremely powerful but heavy on coal. Eight tons on the tender and if 'cracked and stacked' nearer nine: but they were driven like a Great Northern Atlantic, with a long cut-off and plenty of regulator and they thrived on such treatment and were quite economical. But if a driver worked 1470 and her sisters that way (and many did), the fireman would be very, very busy and an onlooker could hear her long before she hove in sight.

I knew a driver who had been a fireman on freight work at Keadby Junction shed, which closed in the 1920s. He transferred to Doncaster and his seniority took him into the Pacific link on A1 4481. He had a heavy-handed driver and they emptied the tender on the 312-mile round trip to King's Cross and back, more than eight tons to be correctly placed over the 41sq ft grate.

The great H.N.Gresley, the Chief Mechanical Engineer of the Great Northern Railway (G.N.) and, after 1923, the L.N.E.R., had not then grasped the importance of using long lap, long travel piston valves and then a much more refined method of driving. The Great Western had long done so and no doubt the 'Great Bear' was a free running, powerful and economical engine, but look at the working conditions for the driver and fireman in that little cab and think of using a shovel in such cramped conditions. But there was a big grate and the fireman would put on an enormous fire before starting, and he might well with good Welsh coal and economical working go halfway to Bristol without touching the fire.

The tender drawing on page 25 is particularly interesting. It shows the scoop, the end of which is lowered into the water trough over which the train is passing at around 60 mph, thus eliminating the need to stop to fill the tank which holds 5,000 gallons. In my day on the A1s during the war, the scoop was lowered into the trough by turning a handle, a relatively easy task, but I see that on the 1922 drawing the chute is lowered by a lever, a very different proposition — as I found out to my cost on a G.N. Atlantic when the lever jammed full open, the driver and I were soaked and the footplate knee-deep in coal brought down by torrents of overflowing water.

In 1921, H.N.Gresley introduced his quintuple articulated train (see page 26), which had a kitchen car with electric fittings and cooking appliances and which worked on the King's Cross and Leeds services! How well I remember those coaches on the 1730 Leeds–King's Cross stripped of all their glory and equipment and packed solid with soldiers and how well I recall that wartime train, immensely long, drawing up two or even three times at Retford and Newark and once at Peterborough and Grantham. At Retford, after the third draw-up, the Grantham A1 would be standing on the turn-out onto the through road and then refuse, time after time, to get away. The last straw would be the stop and restart at Finsbury Park and then, for me, a bus journey in the black-out with the elderly conductor punching the exact hole in the ticket to denote the Baker Street stage. A long day by the time I got home on the midnight from Baker Street.

And then in 1927, Gresley was persuaded by his Technical Assistant, the excellent Bert Spencer, to go over to long travel valves and to full regulator and short cut-off working of the engine so that, instead of the old 40–50%, full regulator and 15–25% was the order of the day. 'Cut-off' means more or less what it says, high pressure steam is cut-off from entering the cylinder when the piston has gone 15% of its stroke and its work is then done by expansion of high pressure steam. Gresley, once converted, had the design and valve setting of all the A1s altered by 1931 and, of course, any new Pacifics or indeed nearly every class of engine turned out from then on.

In 1928 came the non-stop, at 10.00 to and from Edinburgh with the corridor

The 'Flying Scotsman' leaves Kings Cross for the first non-stop run to Edinburgh, 1 May 1928.

tender fitted to selected A1s, including 4472, 'Flying Scotsman' (see page 30), the train of course carrying the same name whichever engine was booked to the job and with crews changing on the move north of York with King's Cross, Gateshead or Haymarket men and in later years, just the Cross and Haymarket. But sometimes it was touch and go for coal and it was very hard for the fireman to fetch and carry and throw fast enough to meet the desire of that raging fire.

The only time I went on the non-stop was in 1958, when I volunteered to go forward to help the Haymarket fireman. Arriving in the cab of the A4 and without more ado, I opened the gate, took the spare blade, walked into the tender and then shovelled and shovelled until all the coal was within easy reach. I shall never forget the Scottish fireman's gratitude when he asked me where I was based and what I did for a living.

And now by way of light relief, how you will enjoy the choppy flight from Croydon to Edinburgh (see page 37) where the speed actually reached 100mph to catch and overtake the wrong train at the Border but finally catching the *Flying Scotsman* itself and telling them to take it easy before heading off at 115mph for Turnhouse Aerodrome. And then a frenzied drive by powerful motor-cars to the Waverley was thwarted by traffic, only to find the 'Scotsman' had got there first!

It is good to read a piece on the work of the Civil Engineers Department (see page 40), for there was always an affinity between the Civils and us Loco Running folk, and we worked particularly closely together when our Stratford 45-ton breakdown crane, foreman and gang and the District Engineer's expert staff were on bridging and electrification work. Their Electrification Engineer, Brian Davis, and our Breakdown Foreman, Syd Casselton, made a marvellously effective pair in charge throughout a hard and continuous weekend.

And then we come to Eric Gill, the famous sculptor and the complete reverse from either Brian or Syd! In January 1933, *The Railway Magazine* published a similar paragraph to that on page 46 but included the names of the group. Gill Sans was to become the standard public presentation of the printed word on the L.N.E.R., the headboard carried on the engine working the *Flying Scotsman* being a case in point. Eric Gill was invited late in 1932 to place the name-board in position on the A1 Pacific before departure from platform 10. He was a remarkable man, who must have persuaded his hosts to grant him a footplate pass to ride to Grantham at a later date, for the group included Mr I.S.W. Groom, the Locomotive Running Supt. Hence the interesting, amusing and, on the whole, pretty accurate piece but with certain eccentricities! The personalities are Eric Gill, Mr Groom, J.F.Sparke, District Locomotive Running Supt at King's Cross, the Station Master squeezed into the background despite his 'Topper', O.H.Corble, a senior L.N.E.R. Commercial Officer and Charles Dandridge, the Advertising Manager, all of them apart from Mr Gill and the Station Master wearing various shapes and sizes of bowler hat.

Gill's introduction to the train crew on the day of his footplate trip began with the arrival in his van of the very smart guard and if you read P.G.Wodehouse, you will recognise Gill as a species of Bertie Wooster! Once installed in the private world of the footplate on the last A1 2582 to be built and in charge of Gateshead Driver Young, he was offered the fireman's seat and, a changed man, marvelled at the enginemen's work, which you must take with a small pinch of salt particularly when the fireman was said to be highly skilled with the shovel but spilt coal on the cab floor with every charge! Gill's contribution was to sound the whistle approaching and passing Peterborough and what a perfect description of that simple task! The G.N. whistle had always been a poor affair when compared with the hoarse but melodious Great Central pattern and the imperiously clear blast of a small and self-important Great Eastern engine.

On the L.N.E.R., the years 1934–39 showed a gradual improvement in the state of the country from the terrible days of the slump that affected the lives of so many redundant railwaymen but who were recalled to deal with the enormous burden shouldered by our railwaymen throughout the war. In 1934, the L.N.E.R. had begun to give serious thought to very fast running on the G.N. main line, which culminated with the amazing work of 'Mallard' reaching 126 mph in 1938 with old Joe Duddington of Doncaster sitting imperturbably at the throttle and his fireman, Tommy Bray, bailing it in as if his life depended on it.

However in 1934, it was the turn of 4472 (see page 50) and its regular crew, Bill Sparshatt and fireman R.Webster, to achieve a record which would be beaten a year later by the same crew but with an A3 Pacific, 2750. In the photograph on page 53, Sparshatt is, about to do the outside oiling, which is fair enough but if you look closely, you will see that he has no overall trousers on and to a loco man, this means only one thing—that he won't be going underneath to fill the middle big-end and his fireman has to do the job. And that smart youngish fireman shovelled nine tons of coal to cover 41 sq ft of grate for that day's work. Sparshatt therefore had a certain reputation. On this occasion, the four coach train left platform 11 at King's Cross and had to pass through some curvature limited to 8 mph for many years after. However, Sparshatt set off hell for leather, lurching into Gas Works tunnel and frightening the daylights out of Cecil J. Allen and others in the train and in the know. Of course, very few engines had speedometers in those days indeed for many years afterwards, but they passed Finsbury Park in four seconds under four minutes at the unheard speed of nearly 60 mph.

But it was not always like that, for the war brought fast running to a halt and a limitation to 60 mph with tremendous loads. In fact, whereas 4472 had but four coaches, driver Bill Carman of Grantham with an A4 2509 needed 16 minutes with 25 coaches to struggle up Holloway Bank and pass Finsbury Park. But imagine this: no platform at King's Cross (or anywhere else) could take a train of 25 coaches and the front twelve would be in another platform full of passengers to be pulled forward and then backed on to the rest of the train and with the driver quite unable to see his distances from the blackness of the tunnel. Nor could the fireman allow the engine to blow off steam within the confines of the low tunnel roof under the Regent's Canal: the heat would have been terrible yet he had to have a fire big and hot enough to meet the huge demands for steam once they got the right-away. And how could that be given, with the guard way back in the train and the corridors jam-packed with luggage and bodies. The ever resourceful railwaymen of all grades shrugged and got on with the job, but for Driver Carman and his mate, it must have been hell on earth starting away in that tunnel.

On page 61 there are Rules 186–196 governing wrong line working due to

R.H.N. Hardy driving 4498 class A4 'Sir Nigel Gresley', on the Settle and Carlisle line, 10 October 1978, when the locomotive was travelling at around 70mph.

track repairs or obstructions on up or down lines. But the relevant rules are 186 to 208, so I recommend the reader to search on the internet for the report of the accident that took place at Barby between Rugby Central and Braunston & Willoughby on the Great Central main line on August 7 1955. In charge of a V2 class locomotive working the 1035 Manchester to Marylebone from Leicester was driver Charlie Simpson of Neasden who, with his father, had done a great deal for me when I was younger. The report, especially the conclusions, is really worth reading, fully, clearly and humanely explained but to me, very sad.

The Walschaert's Valve gear (see page 68) was introduced in about 1879 in this country. Here again are questions and answers along with excellent diagrams of the gear in position and its derivation from the middle cylinder along with the parts of the 2 to 1 gear in position. Enginemen are instructed as to how various parts of the gear can be removed in the event of failure, but my advice would be to speak to control at once and get the Running Shed fitters on the job pronto. They know how it can be done and how best to move a badly crippled engine!

Jack Peckston of Copley Hill, was a comical man who drove 4472 from King's Cross to Leeds on her last journey in the service of BR, and thereon she was 'Pegler's engine' regularly at work all over the country until the disastrous American trip.

Ossie Nock (see page 85) was a distinguished railway author who understood railway work. Here, he has taken us down the G.N. main line and over other main lines where 4472 almost always distinguished herself. Once you can fire a wide firebox through the trap door and the driver knows what is what, you can do great work. Not always, particularly in the war and with the A1 2549, when we had 19 coaches, we struggled over Stoke summit with less than 100 lbs of steam, the water 'down in't gob 'oil', the engine in full gear and the regulator wide open, at about 15 mph a very rough trip indeed. These things happen to everybody, even to the likes of the 'Mallard' and in the 71 years that I handled a shovel, we stopped 18 times and, on one occasion in 1944, three times between Sheffield and Dunford Bridge, with a K3 and a boiler full of soap-suds. Experience!

Ossie was present on the non-stop in May 1968 but I was missing, as my

R.H.N. Hardy firing, at a mere 63 years old, on 4498 class A4 'Sir Nigel Gresley'. Tea cans can be seen on the tray and Vic Waites, the driver, has the regulator well open and is driving with a short cut-off, and economically.

wife and I were house-hunting in Wirral, for I was to become Divisional Manager in Liverpool. Les Richards was Chief Locomotive Inspector of the N.E. Region and, on retirement, ran 4472 for Alan Pegler (see page 77) when she was based at Carnforth and he was behind much of her wonderful work over the Settle–Carlisle road. As Divisional Manager at King's Cross, Alan Pegler knew my pedigree, for he had been on the Eastern Region Board. At York HQ, the Assistant General Manager (A.G.M.) Technical wanted nothing to do with steam or Pegler: the phone rang and Alan asked me whether 4472 could do the non-stop. Of course it would with six to seven coaches and water troughs and light handling, and I fell for it. The next phone call was from York and the AGM gave me a friendly roasting, for he was an old steam-man himself.

And then George Hinchcliffe (see page 109), one of the best, who was Alan

Pegler's front man. George's obituary says it all and unwittingly he did me a very good turn. I was one of a long, long list of speakers at Bill McAlpine's 70th, but George went on and on and left us all bereft of words and Judy (Lady McAlpine) came over and asked us if we would mind stepping down! George went to America with the engine and then brought her home to her new owner. And I remember the day she set off for Derby driven by George Bernard Shaw of Edge Hill, Liverpool!

From January 1987 to January 1993, I was Chairman of the Steam Locomotive Operators Association (S.L.O.A.). I had retired from British Rail (B.R.) in December 1982 and some folk thought it would do good to have a retired railwayman in charge. But during that period, 4472 went to Australia (see page 120) with Roland Kennington and Dave Rollin (ex B.R.) of Flying Scotsman Services and what a marvellous show they all put up. In S.L.O.A. we had Bernard Staite in charge of operations and in charge of Special Trains on B.R. we had David Ward, whom I had known for years. The 'Scotsman' came home, had a thorough going-over and carried on as before and I had my last journey on her in 2005.

You will now read some of the inside story of what took place and of the difficulties that lay ahead. I would love to see her at work again, but if she is going to pay her way, there are some highly successful modifications made in her later years of service that should be retained. I will say no more, but I am all the happier for having fired and driven the old engine many times — and never a bad trip.

R.H.N. Hardy
June 2013

Publishers Notes.

1. In this anthology, references to material not included in a selected extract have been removed to avoid confusion, unless they are an integral part of a sentence. In these instances the note [not included here] has been added.

2. In the compiling of this book the publishers have referred throughout to the locomotive as the 'Flying Scotsman'. In the event that the route or service is detailed this is referred to as the *Flying Scotsman*.

British 'Pacific' Locomotives Compared.

(Taken from The Railway Magazine *July 1922)*

Here are three 'Pacific' locomotives, powerful and impressive, two of which were to disappear from the scene, and the other which would be developed stage by stage, to become a world-beater. Look at them closely before you read the coming chapters and you will surely pick the ultimate winner.

In view of the special interest attaching to the Great Western and Great Northern "Pacific" locomotives, and in response to requests, the following particulars of the Great Western "Pacific" locomotive No. 111, *The Great Bear*, and the Great Northern "Pacific" No. 1470, described fully last month are given in parallel columns, together with those of Sir Vincent Raven's corresponding engine, now under construction for the North Eastern Railway :–

	G.W.R No. 111.	G.N.R. No. 1470.	N.E.R Under construction
Cylinders	15 in. × 26 in. (4)	20 in. × 26 in. (3)	19 in. × 26 in. (3)
Coupled wheels	6 ft. 8½ in. diam.	6 ft. 8½ in. diam.	6 ft. 8 in.
Bogie wheels	3 ft. 2 in. diam.	3 ft. 2 in. diam.	3 ft. 1¼ in.
Trailing wheels	3 ft. 8 in. diam.	3 ft. 8 in. diam.	3 ft. 9¼ in.
Steam pressure	225 lb. per sq. in.	180 lb. per sq. in.	200 lb. per sq. in.
Heating surface–			
Tubes	2,596.97 sq. ft.	2,715 sq. ft.	2,211.2 sq. ft.
Firebox	158.51 sq. ft.	215 sq. ft.	211 sq. ft.
Superheater	505.77 sq. ft.	525 sq. ft.	695.6 sq. ft.
Total	3,261.25 sq. ft.	3,455 sq. ft.	3,117.8 sq. ft.
Grate area	41.79 sq. ft.	41.25 sq. ft.	41 sq. ft.
Couple wheelbase	14 ft.	14 ft. 6 in.	15 ft.
Total wheelbase, engine	34 ft. 6 in.	35 ft. 9 in.	37 ft 2 in.
Total wheelbase, engine and tender	61 ft. ½ in.	60 ft 10⅝ in.	61 ft. 11¾ in.
Weight on bogie wheels	19 tons 18 cwt.	17 tons 1 cwt.	19 tons.*
Weight on leading coupled wheels	18 tons.	24 tons.	20 tons.*
Weight on middle coupled wheels	18 tons.	20 tons.	20 tons.*
Weight on trailing coupled wheels	18 tons.	20 tons.	20 tons.*
Weight on trailing wheels	17 tons 8 cwt.	15 tons 8 cwt.	18 tons.*
Total weight of engine in working order	97 tons.	92 tons 9 cwt.	97 tons.*
Weight of tender loaded	45 tons. 19 cwt.	56 tons 6 cwt.	46 tons 2 cwt.
Total weight of engine and tender	142 tons 15 cwt.	148 tons 15 cwt.	143 tons 2 cwt.*

* Estimated weights.

By the courtesy of Sir Vincent Raven, K.B.E., Chief Mechanical Engineer, North Eastern Railway, we are also enabled to reproduce an outline dimensioned drawing of the 4-6-2 locomotive now being built at Darlington to his designs. Additional interest attaches to these new engines, of which two are to be constructed, inasmuch as they are intended for fast passenger traffic on the East Coast route, and on completion will work in conjunction with the new engines of the same type on the Great Northern Railway. Furthermore, both are of the 3-cylinder single-expansion type, but, whereas in the case of the Great Northern engine the cylinders drive the middle pair of coupled wheels, in the new North Eastern Railway locomotive they drive the leading pair, the cranks being set 120 deg. apart. Sir Vincent Raven's new engine is remarkable for its proportional characteristics. The boiler has an outside diameter of 6 ft. (or 6 ft. 3½ in. outside clothing), the length between tube plates being 21 ft. It carries a working pressure of 200 lb. per sq. in., and has a total heating surface of 3, 117.8 sq. ft. Three safety-valves are mounted one behind the other above the firebox.

The diagram shows the general appearance of the engine and tender, giving the estimated weights and leading dimensions, etc. The cylinders, as already stated, are three in number,

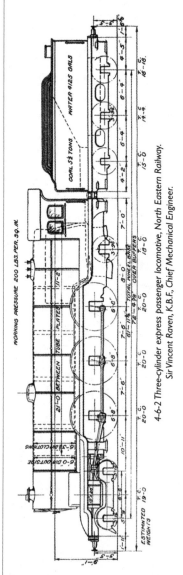

4-6-2 Three-cylinder express passenger locomotive, North Eastern Railway.
Sir Vincent Raven, K.B.E., Chief Mechanical Engineer.

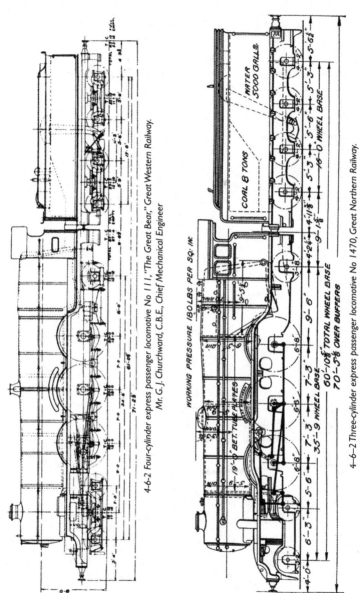

4-6-2 Four-cylinder express passenger locomotive No 111, "The Great Bear," Great Western Railway.
Mr. G. J. Churchward, C.B.E., Chief Mechanical Engineer

4-6-2 Three-cylinder express passenger locomotive No 1470, Great Northern Railway.
Mr. H.N. Gresley, C.B.E., Chief Mechanical Engineer.

each 19 in. in diameter by 26 in. stroke. The cylinders and steam chests are in one casting, the steam chests being common to all, while the three exhaust chambers are separate to the bottom of the blast pipe, where they combine. The cylinders are fitted with piston valves 8¾ in. in diameter, and the valve gear – Stephenson's link motion – is applied direct to each of the cylinders. The driving wheels are 6 ft. 8 in. in diameter, and the rigid wheelbase 15 ft., the total wheelbase for the engine being 37 ft. 2in.

The bogie wheels are 3 ft. 1¼ in. in diameter, and arranged on a wheelbase of 6 ft. 6 in.; carrying wheels 3 ft. 9¼ in. in diameter are employed, these being fitted with radial axle-boxes with a side movement of 3½ in. The boiler is fitted with a round-topped firebox casing. The tubes are 2¼ in. in diameter, and the smoke tubes 5¼ in. in diameter. There are 118 of the former, and 24 of the latter, with superheating elements. The firebox casing is 8 ft. long by 6 ft. 5 in. at the bottom, the actual grate area being 41 sq. ft., the firebox is extended into the barrel of the boiler, and its outline is shown in the diagram, its overall length being 11 ft. 2 in. The effect of this extension has been to reduce the length of tubes and increases the firebox heating surface, whilst it further acts as an additional combustion chamber.

The distribution of heating surface is as follows :–

	Sq. ft.			Sq. ft.
Ordinary tubes	1,517.6		Superheater tubes	693.6
Superheater elements	695.6		Firebox	211
		Total	3,117.8	
Grate area	41			

The tenders are of the self-trimming type, carrying 5½ tons of coal and 4,125 gallons of water. They are six-wheeled, having a wheelbase of 12 ft. 8 in. The combined wheelbase of the engine and tender is 61 ft. 11¾ in., and the length over buffers overall 72ft. 4⅜ in. The weights are given in the diagram, from which it will be seen that the weight available for adhesion is 60 tons, while the total of engine and tender in working order is 143 tons 2 cwt.

The engine develops a tractive effort at 85 per cent. of boiler pressure, of 29,918lb. It will be noted that according to the estimated weights, each pair of coupled wheels supports 20 tons, thus affording 60 tons of adhesion, and giving an adhesive factor of 4.49.

L.N.E.R. EXPRESS PASSENGER ENGINE
4–6–2 PACIFIC TYPE 4472
'FLYING SCOTSMAN'

Constructed in the Company's works
at Doncaster 1922 to the designs of

**MR. H.N. GRESLEY, C.B.E., M.I.C.E., M.I.M.E., M.I.E.E. Chief Mechanical Engineer
and exhibited at the BRITISH EMPIRE EXHIBITION WEMBLEY 1924**

*(Taken from L.N.E.R. exhibition catalogue for the British Empire Exhibition
Wembly 1924)*

LOCOMOTIVE No. 4472 is one of twelve three-cylinder simple expansion Pacific type Locomotives now in service on the Main Lines of the London and North Eastern Railway, and of which the construction of a further forty will be completed during 1924 in the Company's Locomotive Workshops and by outside Locomotive Builders.

These Locomotives were designed by Mr. H. N. GRESLEY, Chief Mechanical Engineer of the London and North Eastern Railway Company, and were introduced for working the fastest and heaviest Express Passenger trains between London and Edinburgh. The first engines were put into service in 1922.

The principal dimensions and ratios are given below :–

Grate—	Length	5′ 10″ ¹⁵⁄₁₆	1*m* 802
	Width	6′ 11¾″	2*m* 127
	Grate Area	41.25 sq. ft.	3*m* 283
Firebox—	Height of crown		
	above } Front	6′ 8″ ¹³⁄₁₆	2*m* 053
	foundation ring } Back	6′ 0″ ⁹⁄₁₆	1*m* 837
	Interior, length at top	7′ 11¾″	2*m* 432
	" width at boiler centre	5′ 4½″	1*m* 638
	Thickness of } Sides and back	⁹⁄₁₆″	14*mm* 3
	copper plates } Tubeplate	⁹⁄₁₆″ and 1″	14*mm* 3 and 25*mm* 4
Boiler—	Outside length firebox, overall	9′ 5½″	2*m* 883
	at bottom	6′ 8″	2*m* 032
	width	7′ 9″	2*m* 362

Diameter of barrel (maximum)		6' 5"	1m 956
Length of barrel		19' 0"	5m 791
Thickness of barrel plates		5/8" and 11/16"	15mm 9 and 17mm 5
Thickness of wrapper plates		9/16"	14mm 3
Outside diameter of smokebox		6' 0"	1m 829
Outside length of smokebox		5' 11"	1m 803

Tubes (small) —

Material	Steel.	
Number	168	
Diameter outside	2¼"	57mm 2
Thickness	10 I.W.G. —0.128 ins.	3mm 25

Tubes (superheater flue) —

Number	32	
Diameter outside	5¼"	133mm 4
Thickness	5/32"	4mm
Length between tubeplates	19' 0"	5m 791

Heating Surface —

Firebox	215 sq. ft.	19m 297
Tubes 2¼" diameter	1880 "	174m 266
Flues 5¼" diameter	835 "	77m 257
Total evaporative	— —	— — — —
heating surface	2930	272 m 22

Superheater —

No. of elements	32	
Diameter inside	1¼"	31mm 75
Heating surface	525 sq. ft.	48.78
Total heating	— —	— — — —
surface	3455 "	320 m 298

Two "Ross" Pop Safety Valves	4" diameter	101mm 6
Working Pressure	180 lbs. per sq. in.	12.6 kg/cm2
Boiler Horse Power	1815	

			DIAMETER	LENGTH
Axles. —	Journals	Bogie	6½", 165mm 1	9", 228mm 6
		Coupled wheels	9½", 341mm 3	11", 279mm 4
		Trailing wheels	6", 152mm 4	11", 279mm 4
	Crank Pins – Outside		5½", 139mm 7	6", 152mm 4

	Inside	8¼", 209mm 6	6", 152mm 4
Coupling Pins –	Leading	4", 101mm 6	4½", 114mm 3
	Driving	6", 152mm 4	4¼", 108mm
	Trailing	4", 101mm 6	4½", 114mm 3
	266mm 7 128mm 6		

Springs– Bogie helical 10½" long free 5" ¹⁄₁₆ outside diameter "Timmis" section. 1m 067

Coupled Wheels laminated 3' 6" centres.

11 plates 5" wide x ⅝" thick.

127mm 15mm 9

1m 372

Trailing Wheels laminated 4' 6" centres.

11 plates 5" wide × ⅝" thick.

127mm 15mm 9

Cylinders – Number	3	
Diameter	20"	508mm
Stroke	26"	660mm 4

Cylinder Horse Power 1946

Motion — Type	Outside	Walschaert	
	Inside	Gresley	
Type of valves		Piston	
Diameter of valves		8"	203mm 2
Maximum travel of valves		4" ⁹⁄₁₆	115mm 9
Steam lap		1¼"	31mm 8
Exhaust lap		–¼"	6mm 4
Cut-off in full gear		65%	

Tractive Effort at 85% Boiler pressure 29,835 lbs. 13,533 *kg.*

Total Adhesive Weight 134,400 lbs. 60,981 *kg.*

Ratio – Adhesive Weight ÷ Tractive Effort 4.5

BOILER

The boiler is shown in detail in Figs, 10, 11 and 12 [not shown here].

The boiler is of the wide firebox type, with the firebox carried over the frame.

The inner firebox is made of copper, all other plates being Acid Open Hearth Mild Steel. In order to increase the firebox volume and to allow shorter tubes to be used, the firebox is extended into the barrel to form a combustion chamber.

The staying is also improved by this arrangement.

The steel wrapper plate of the firebox is in one piece and is attached to the boiler barrel by a double riveted lap joint, and to the throat plate by a single riveted lap joint, the throat plate being attached to the boiler by a double riveted lap joint.

The first course of the boiler is conical, the second course being parallel, and connected by a double riveted lap joint.

The dome is blocked from one piece of plate, and double riveted to the boiler, with a stiffening plate inside.

The longitudinal seams of the boiler barrel are quadruple riveted with double butt strips, as shown in Fig. 12. [not shown here].

The back plate is fastened to the wrapper by a single riveted lap joint.

The firebox is in three plates, the wrapper, throat, and back plates. Single riveted lap joints are used throughout.

The firehole is made by the flanging of both steel and copper back plates into contact, and riveting together.

The staying of the firebox sides and ends is by copper stays, the combustion chamber being radially stayed.

The roof stays are direct stays of steel.

Transverse stays are provided over the top of the firebox, and longitudinal stays from the end plates to the top of the boiler.

A manhole is provided underneath the boiler near the throat plate for examination and cleaning.

A steam distribution box behind the safety valve supplies steam to the various fittings.

The back part of the grate is horizontal and the front part is sloped down. A drop grate is provided in the forward sloping part of the grate.

The boiler is supported at the front end on a cast steel saddle. At the middle it rests freely on a frame stay.

The firebox foundation ring rests on a frame stay at front end, and on supports at the back end, with shoes on part of the foundation ring to act as rubbing surfaces. The firebox is held down by a vertical plate which allows freedom for expansion.

SUPERHEATER

The superheater fitted is of the Robinson type and the 32 elements are provided with shorter return bends than is common practice.

The anti-vacuum valve is fitted above the smokebox and connects direct to the header as shown in Fig. 3, [not shown here], so that the cold air is drawn through the elements when steam is shut off to prevent overheating.

LAGGING

The barrel is lagged with Wadnit blocks and asbestos mattresses on the firebox.

FRAMES

The frames are of Acid Open Hearth Steel 1⅛" thick. The frames are held together at the front end by the buffer beam and by the inside cylinders, and suitable cast steel frame stays distributed along its length, with a cast steel drag box at the back end.

BOGIE

The bogie is of the swing link type.

RADIAL AXLEBOX

The radial axleboxes of the trailing pair of wheels are of the "Cortazzi" pattern, giving a side movement of 2½", and are shown in Fig. 24 [not shown here].

WHEELS

The wheels are of cast steel with tyres of Class "C" steel on the driving wheels and Class "D" on the others.

The diameter of the driving and coupled wheels is 6' 8".

The tyres are bored with a shrinkage allowance of 1/800th of the inside diameter, and the driving tyres are further secured by turned rivets.

AXLES

The axles are of forged steel made by the Acid Open Hearth process.

The crank axle is of the built-up type, and has extended webs to balance the crank itself. The crank axle is built up of five pieces.

BALANCING

The engine has the respective revolving weights balanced in each wheel.

Sixty per cent. of the weight of the reciprocating parts is balanced.

The reciprocating weight for the middle cylinder is balanced in the driving wheels; that for the outer cylinders is equally divided among the six coupled wheels.

SANDING

Steam sanding is fitted to the leading and driving coupled wheels.

CYLINDER COCKS

Cylinder waste water cocks with relief valves are fitted and are operated by a "Bowden" wire control gear.

INJECTORS

A live Gresham & Craven 11*mm* steam injector is used on the right-hand side of the engine. An exhaust injector of Davis & Metcalf's manufacture is provided on the left-hand side.

SUSPENSION

The engine is suspended independently at each axle. Helical springs are used on the bogie and the driving wheels, and laminated on the leading and trailing coupled wheels, the trailing carrying wheels and the tender wheels.

CYLINDERS

The three cylinders drive the middle coupled axle.

PISTON AND ROD

The piston and rod is combined as shown in Fig. 16 [not shown here], the rod being hollow, and is made of high tensile heat-treated Nickel Chrome steel. The cast-iron piston rings are contained in a bronze rim cast round the piston head.

CROSS HEAD

A cross head with "T" shape slide is fitted working between three bars, as shown in Figs. 3 and 13 [not shown here].

PISTON ROD AND VALVE SPINDLE ROD PACKING

Cast-iron packing is fitted in the piston rod and valve spindle stuffing boxes.

RODS

The connecting and coupling rods are made of high tensile heat-treated Nickel Chrome steel of 50 tons per sq. inch tensile with a yield point of 80 per cent. of the tensile strength. The outside connecting rod is shown in Fig.17 [not shown here].

VALVE DISTRIBUTION

The valve gear, seen in Figs. 13, 14 (right) and 15 [not shown here], is of the Walschaert type in the case of the outside cylinders. The inside cylinder valve is operated indirectly on the principle devised by Mr. Gresley, and already in use on a number of locomotives. This arrangement involves two horizontal rocking levers connected with the outside cylinder-valve tail rods. These levers are of unequal length. The longer has two unequal arms respectively 4ft.^{11}⁄$_{16}$ in. and 2ft.^{11}⁄$_{32}$ in. long between centres; the shorter has two equal arms 1ft. ½in. long. Each lever is coupled at one end to its valve spindle by a short link. The long lever is pivoted on a fixed point; the short one is pivoted on the short arm of the long. The second end of the short lever drives the valve spindle of the inside cylinder by means of a long link. Roller bearings are fitted to the large lever at the fulcrum-pin and pivot-pin of the short lever. The arrangement will be clear from Fig. 14, which shows details of the gear.

REVERSING GEAR

The reversing of the engine is by the aid of a screw with hand-wheel, the gear being fitted with ball bearings and with a power lock operated by the vacuum maintained for the brake. At the same time a ferodo-lined clutch worked by the vacuum comes into action on the weigh bar shaft.

SAFETY VALVES

Two 4" Ross pattern pop safety valves are fitted.

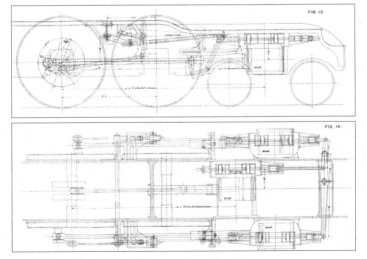

Valve distribution, Figures 13 and 14.

REGULATOR

The steam regulator is of the Lockyer type. It is worked by an inverted lever on each side of the firebox, fitted on a cross-shaft which passes through two stuffing boxes in a mounting enclosing a short arm coupled to the regulator rod. It is clearly shown in Fig. 17 [not shown here].

The regulator rod is in perfect end balance.

STEAM CHEST PRESSURE GAUGE

A pressure gauge showing the pressure of steam in the steam chest is fitted in the cab on the Driver's side.

LUBRICATION

The cylinder lubrication is by means of a Detroit hydrostatic sight feed lubricator; the axleboxes are lubricated by Wakefield mechanical force feed lubricators.

BRAKE

The engine is fitted with the Automatic Vacuum Brake acting on the coupled wheels of the engine and on all the tender wheels.

The vacuum gauge is fitted on the Driver's side, near to the steam chest pressure gauge.

STEAM HEATING

The engine is fitted with steam heating pipes and couplings.

TENDER

The General Arrangement of the Tender is shown in Figs. 18, 19, 20, 21 and 22.

The tender is carried on four pairs of wheels, holds 5,000 gallons of water and 8 tons of coal.

It is fitted with water pick-up gear, lever operated, and water gauge, and with hand brake.

The coal space is self-trimming, the back and sides sloping sufficiently to allow the coal to work down to the shovel plate.

Rubber draw springs are fitted.

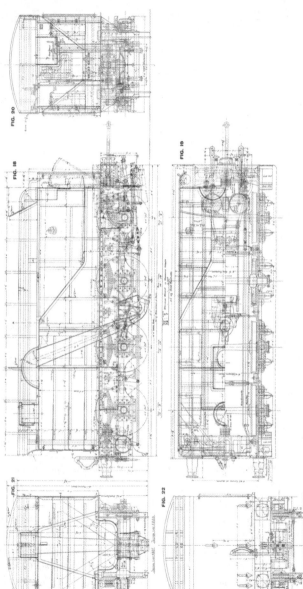

FIGS. 18, 19, 20, 21 & 22.

FIG. 20

FIG. 18

FIG. 19

FIG. 21

FIG. 22

The Tender, Figures 18, 19, 20, 21 and 22.

New Rolling-Stock for Day East Coast Trains, L.N.E.R.

(Taken from The Railway Magazine *July 1924)*

It was always a pleasure to travel in Gresley or Thompson's main line stock for years after both men had passed on. One must not forget the burden born by the passenger stock during the last War, often bursting with humanity, luggage and kit – and comfort where none was expected.

Some three years ago Mr. H.N. Gresley, then Chief Mechanical Engineer of the Great Northern Railway, placed in service on the King's Cross and Leeds route a quintuple "articulated" train of which a special feature was a kitchen car entirely equipped with electric cooking appliances. This train, described and illustrated in the RAILWAY MAGAZINE for December, 1921, has obtained so high a reputation in service that, in preparing designs for new sets of vehicles for the day Anglo-Scottish trains on the East Coast route, an all-electric kitchen car arranged to serve first and third-class restaurant cars on either side to form a 'Triplet' articulated restaurant-car unit was decided upon as a distinctive feature. Four of the new trains are being placed in service, and the two already completed began to run on October 1 on the 10 a.m. from King's Cross, the *Flying Scotsman*, and the corresponding train from Edinburgh. It is expected that the two other trains will be available in November for use on the 1.15 p.m. from King's Cross to Edinburgh and the equivalent south-bound train.

Each complete train, which has been built at Doncaster to the designs of Mr. H.N. Gresley, C.B.E., Chief Mechanical Engineer, London and North Eastern Railway, includes 12 vehicles. Apart from the "Triplet" restaurant-car set, the make-up varies somewhat, owing to the necessity for providing through sections to and from different destinations north of Edinburgh and the particular requirements of the respective trains. It is mainly for this reason, in fact, that the articulated principle is not applied throughout the train.

The ordinary vehicles in the train correspond substantially with standard East Coast designs, except that many detail improvements are included, and advantage has been taken of all good features to be obtained from the rolling-stock practices of the companies now included in the London and North Eastern Railway. It is further of interest to note that these are the first complete restaurant-car trains for an important service constructed since the formation of the London and North

Train of new rolling-stock on trial run, September 29 1924.

Eastern Railway, though many individual vehicles have been added to stock since the new company was formed. It is claimed that these new trains are the most comfortable and luxurious in the world for passengers paying ordinary fares.

A trial run of one of the trains for the 10 a.m. services was made on Monday, September 29, the train then consisting of the following vehicles :–

| | Length over Buffers. | | Weight. | |
	Ft.	In.	Tons.	Cwts.
Third brake	58	6	27	10
Luggage brake van	55	0	26	10
Compo.	60	0	34	10
Compo.	60	0	34	10
Third	60	0	34	5
"Triplet" set	153	7	83	0
Compo.	60	0	34	10
Compo.	60	0	34	10
Third	60	0	34	5
Luggage brake van	55	0	26	10
Totals	68	21	370	0

The tendency in recent years in the decoration of restaurant cars and other railway carriages has been to make them more and more ornate. This is particularly noticeable on the railways abroad, but in dealing with the scheme of decoration for the new train this tendency has been entirely reversed. The prevailing note of the whole scheme of decoration throughout the train is simplicity. The walls of the first-class restaurant car are lined with large naturally coloured mahogany panels. The usual net racks and hat pegs are all of the plainest possible design. The seats in the first-class compartments are of the arm-chair type, comfortably upholstered in green morocco leather, fitted with specially constructed cushions. The floor is covered with green india-rubber over felt, which deadens sound and is very soft to walk on. Further, the rubber floor can be very easily cleaned. The lobbies are covered with cocoa fibre mats. Seats in the third-class compartments are also very comfortably upholstered in crimson and black plush.

Throughout the compartments of the train the electric lighting is under the control of passengers. Special attention has been paid to the lavatory accommodation. Hot and cold water is provided, and the floors are covered with red rubber. All the lavatories can be quickly swabbed out by the staff, the waste water running out by a special arrangement in the floor. A special item of interest in connection with the new trains is the automatic coupling of the Buck-eye type and the Pullman vestibule. The Buck-eye coupling, which was first adopted by the L.N.E.R., holds the carriages rigid, and has proved its efficacy on the sleeping car and other trains by the East Coast route.

The "Triplet" restaurant-car set has sufficient capacity to meet the needs of the entire train. The restaurant cars together enable 78 passengers to be served at the same time, or substantially 25 per cent, of all travelling. With so liberal accommodation it should be possible under normal conditions to meet the needs of every passenger in this respect in two or, at most, three relays. The fact that the entire cooking equipment in the kitchen car is electrical enables space to be conserved to a degree which is hardly practicable when gas or coal stoves are used, while the conditions under which the kitchen staff work are much more pleasant and hygienic, with corresponding advantage both to staff and passengers.

The interior of first-class restaurant car on the new L.N.E.R. east coast train.

The first-class restaurant car on the Flying Scotsman.

LOCOMOTIVE TENDER WITH
SIDE CORRIDOR L.N.E.R.

Designed to permit of Changing Engine Crews during Non-Stop Runs between London (Kings's Cross) and Edinburgh (Waverley)

(Taken from The Railway Gazette *13 April 1928)*

The popularity of the non-stop run to Newcastle, which was a feature of the East Coast Anglo-Scottish services last year, made it clear that there is a considerable public demand for improvements of that kind, and the London and North Eastern Railway have for some time been exploring the possibility of extending the distance covered without stopping. It was felt that the limit of the powers of a single engine crew had been reached, and that it was undesirable on grounds of safety to carry two crews on one engine. Some method had, therefore, to be devised by means of which engine crews could be changed en route, and the provision of a corridor on the tender supplied the solution to the problem.

This has now been carried into effect, and two of Mr. Gresley's three cylinder Pacific-type engines, i.e., 4472 'Flying Scotsman' and 4476 *Royal Lancer*, have been fitted with the new tenders. These will be employed for inaugurating the new London-Edinburgh non-stop runs commencing on May 1, and eight other engines of the same class will be similarly equipped. The driver and fireman in charge on leaving London will be relieved as the train passes Tollerton, 197½ miles from King's Cross, or, roughly, half-way on the journey, the off-duty crew riding in the foremost third-class compartment in the train. On reaching the change-over point the relief crew will pass through the brake van next the engine, and by means of the vestibule connection with the tender, enter the corridor leading to the footplate, those coming off duty passing back to the train in a similar manner.

The advantages to the travelling public of enjoying an uninterrupted run of 392.7 miles are supplemented by other advantages of a kind which favour the locomotive workings. Fewer engines will be required, thus resulting in a corresponding reduction in stand-by losses, while improved engine mileage will be obtained, and by restricting the two crews to the one engine it may be anticipated that better working results will be secured.

Arrangement of Side Corridor.

The necessity of using a good class of coal on a run of this magnitude is ob-

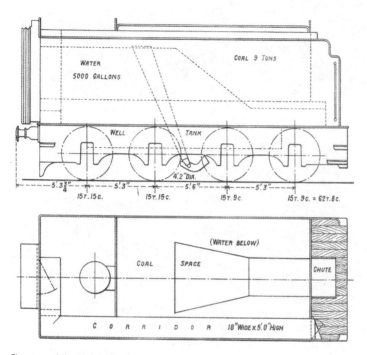

Elevation and sketch plan of tender.

vious, and a point in this connection is that the engines are equipped with shaking grates. The gangway, or corridor, is located on the right-hand side of the tender looking forward, and entirely covered in. It has a width of 18in. and a height of 5 ft. Steps at each end of the tender afford access from the level of the gangway or corridor to that of the engine footplate at the front and the vestibule flooring at the rear. Circular windows are provided, one at each end of the corridor, for lighting the interior, and the position of these

can be seen in some of the accompanying illustrations. The whole arrangement is neat and compact, and there is not the slightest difficulty in passing from the brake van to the footplate, or vice versa, even when travelling at high speeds.

The tender is of the eight-wheeled pattern with rigid axles, and weighs in working order 62 tons 8 cwt., as compared with 56.5 tons of the original standard tender, the coal capacity of which was, however, 8 tons in place of 9 tons. A door is provided at each end

TOP: *General view of 4–6–2 locomotive fitted with new tender.*
LEFT: *Footplate end of the tender.*
RIGHT: *Corridor opening at rear of the tender.*

of the corridor on the tender. Measures have been taken to counteract the lack of balance due to the empty space formed by the corridor on the right-hand side of the tender by the provision of extra weight on that side below the corridor.

We had the opportunity of travelling a short distance on the locomotive and in the brake van over a system of lines adjoining King's Cross station, the bulk of the distance being on reverse curves and over junctions, and the arrangement appears to work with the utmost freedom and smoothness.

The new non-stop run, of 392.7 miles between London and Edinburgh, which commences on May 1, will be the longest in the world, no locomotive engine in regular service having worked such a mileage before without a stop.

INAUGURAL KING'S CROSS–
EDINBURGH NON-STOP RUNS, L.N.E.R.

These Runs, which figure as Daily Schedules in the ordinary Time-tables, were successfully inaugurated on Tuesday last, and aroused tremendous public interest.

(Taken from The Railway Gazette *4 May 1928)*

Particulars of the new London (King's Cross)–Edinburgh (Waverley) non-stop runs which figure in the current time-table, both public and service, have already been given, while we have also described the corridor tender, the hairdressing saloon, ladies' toilet room, and other novelties associated with the up and down *Flying Scotsmen* expresses.

Scenes at King's Cross and Waverley Stations

On Tuesday morning a tremendous crowd assembled at King's Cross to witness the departure of the train. The Lord Mayor of London, Sir Charles Batho, accompanied by Sir Ralph Wedgwood, Chief General Manager, and Mr. H.N. Gresley, Chief Mechinal Engineer, L.N.E.R., inspected the engine and conversed with the four enginemen. Addressing a Press Association representative, the Lord Mayor said :– "I congratulate the London & North Eastern Railway Company on what is undoubtedly a wonderful achievement. It proves that British railways are not behind any others in the world; in fact, they can not only keep abreast of the times, but, I think, in the sphere of railway work they are always a little ahead of it. I congratulate the drivers and wish them the best of luck."

Similar scenes of enthusiasm were witnessed at the principal intermediate stations, notably York and Newcastle, while at Waverley station the arriving train was greeted with great enthusiasm. Mr. J. Calder, General Manager, Scotland, Mr. C.H. Stemp, Superintendent, and other officers of the Scottish Area, with Mr. A.C. Steamer, Chief Assistant Mechanical Engineer, welcomed the train. Mr. Calder presented the four enginemen with commemorative pocket books. They also received a monetary present subscribed by passengers during the journey.

The departure of the up train was also witnessed by a great crowd, Bailie Hay deputising for the Lord Provost of Edinburgh, accompanied by Mr. Calder and other officers, giving it a formal "send-off." The train was met at King's Cross by another huge crowd, so great, indeed, that it was with difficulty that Mr. William Whitelaw, Chairman, L.N.E.R., and Sir Ralph Wedgwood and Lady Wedgwood, who were accompanied by Mr. W.M. Teasdale, Assistant General Manager, Mr.

Alex. Wilson, Divisional General Manager, Southern Area, Mr. W.G.P. Maclure, Running Superintendent, Southern Area, and others could get to the engine as it stopped. Mr. Whitelaw and Sir Ralph Wedgwood shook hands with the four enginemen, and the former presented them with commemorative pocket books. Speaking to a Press Association representative, Mr. Whitelaw said: "The run has been quite successful. There has been no shortage of water and no shortage of coal. We expect to have shortly on the line about 12 engines of similar capacity."

A First-Hand Description of the Run.

The following account of the down journey is supplied by our Technical Editor, who travelled with the train :–

"The train left King's Cross punctually to time. Departure platform No. 10 was thronged with what is believed to be the largest gathering of the public ever known on any such occasion. The engine was No. 4472 'Flying Scotsman', fitted with the new corridor tender. The train was made up entirely of new stock, including a triple articulated set of two restaurant cars (first and third class), and kitchen car, its tare weight being 386 tons. It was well filled throughout, and the load behind the tender, including passengers and luggage, may safely be computed at 400 tons.

"No intermediate stop occurred en route, and the train arrived at Edinburgh, Waverley, at 6.3 p.m., 12 min. before schedule time. Owing to permanent-way checks in the early part of the run, 2 min. had been lost by the time New Barnet was passed, but this was made up before reaching Hatfield. Permanent-way cautions accounted for 9 min. in all in the course of the run, so that with the 12 min. improvement on schedule, the engine gained 21 min. on its timing. No signal slacks were experienced.

"The greatest interest was shown throughout the trip, not only by railway employees but by the public. The platforms at all the principal stations, and particularly at Doncaster, York and Newcastle, were crowded with interested onlookers as the train passed through.

"Driver A. Pibworth and Fireman W. Goddard, of King's Cross, were in charge of the engine from London to Tollerton, at which point Driver T. Blades and Fireman W. Morris, of Gateshead, relieved them. Locomotive Inspect Bramall was also present on the footplate. No difficulty of any kind was experienced with the engine, both coal and water supplies proving ample. It was estimated that rather more than 2 tons of coal remained on the tender when Edinburgh was reached. Water was picked up at six points *en route*.

Enginemen of Down Train greeted by an Old Driver at King's Cross.

Enginemen of Up Train greeted by Mr. William Whitelaw at King's Cross.

Passengers take advantage of the new L.N.E.R. railway luggage laws which allowed record players and portable wirelesses to be carried as personal luggage, circa 1931.

Sir Charles Batho, Lord Mayor of London, Mr. H.N. Gresley, Driver Pibworth and Mr. W.M. Teasdale at King's Cross.

Hairdresser, Lady Attendant and Newsmen working on Up and Down Flying Scotsman expresses.

Conditions of the Engine.

"The writer had an opportunity of conversing with the relief (Gateshead) engin-emen before they went on duty and the London men after they came off the foot-plate. Driver Pibworth reported an excellent run from King's Cross to Tollerton, the engine being in fine trim. It is evident that the new arrangements are very popular with the men, whilst their opinion of Mr. Gresley's Pacific type engines is a very favourable one.

"Later, by Mr. Gresley's courtesy, the writer was permitted to travel on the foot-plate for a part of the way between Berwick and Edinburgh, in company with that gentleman. Passing through the tender corridor at 60 m.p.h. presented no difficulties, and the writer was greatly impressed by the smooth riding qualities of the engine, its roomy well-arranged footplate, accessibility of cab fittings and controls, and the excellent look-out which, when the large size of the boiler is remembered, is exceptionally good. Although then nearing the end of the run, the driver and fireman seemed as fresh and certainly as clean as when they went on duty. The steam pressure gauge consistently registered 156 lb. per sq. in. with light firing, the engine being notched to 30 per cent. cut-off.

"It was reported that the hairdressing saloon was well patronised during the course of the run, whilst the newspaper and book service was also much appreci-ated. A collection among the passengers for the enginemen realised £10.

"Passing times:—Peterborough, 11.24 a.m.; Grantham, 11.58 a.m.; Doncaster, 12.54; York, 1.37 p.m.; Newcastle, 3.22 p.m.; Berwick, 4.50 p.m.; Edinburgh arrive 6.3 p.m. At Newcastle the train passed through on No. 8 platform road. This is, it is believed, the first occasion on which an express in regular service has been booked to pass Newcastle without stopping. The up *Flying Scotsman* (Edinburgh to London non-stop) was met near Pilmoor Junction (204¼ miles from King's Cross) at 2.2 p.m. Generally speaking, the journey was noteworthy for steadiness of running at an even average speed. The new coaching stock proved in every way satisfactory."

The up train, worked by No. 2580 *Shotover*, fitted with a 220-lb. pressure boiler as well as with a corridor tender, was worked by Driver T. Henderson and Fireman R. McKenzie (Edinburgh) and Driver J. Day and Fireman F. Gray (King's Cross). It passed Berwick at 11.10 a.m., Newcastle at 12.40 p.m., York 2.18 p.m., Doncaster 2.58 p.m., and Grantham at 4.4 p.m., reached King's Cross at 6.12½ p.m.

Shen

and NOW
"THE FLYING SCOTSMAN"
THE WORLD'S MOST FAMOUS TRAIN
1862 ——————— 1930
LONDON AND NORTH EASTERN RAILWAY

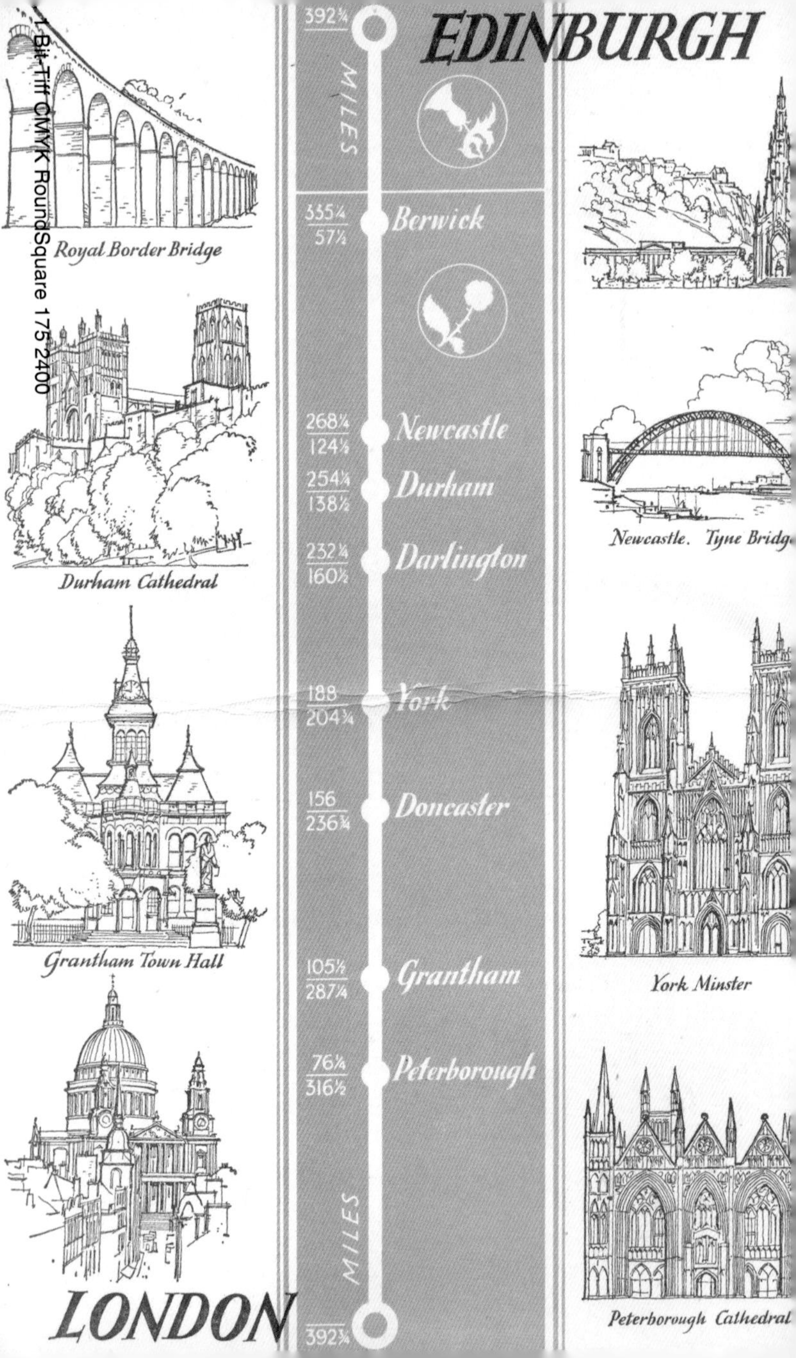
EDINBURGH
392¾
MILES
Royal Border Bridge
335¼
57½
Berwick
Durham Cathedral
268¼
124½
Newcastle
254¼
138½
Durham
232¼
160½
Darlington
Newcastle. Tyne Bridge
188
204¾
York
156
236¾
Doncaster
Grantham Town Hall
105½
287¼
Grantham
York Minster
76¼
316½
Peterborough
MILES
LONDON
392¾
Peterborough Cathedral

SPOTTING THE *FLYING SCOTSMAN*

By Imperial Airways Pilot Captain GORDON P. OLLY

(*Taken from* London & North Eastern Railway Magazine *July 1928*)

[On June 15, by co-operation with the Imperial Airways a comparison was arranged between the "down" non-stop *Flying Scotsman* and an air liner of the latest type named the "City of Glasgow."

Below we print a breezy little article by the pilot of the aeroplane, Captain Gordon P. Olly, explaining how he crossed the Border with the "Junior Scotsman" instead of accompanying the "10 o'clock."]

We had a talk about your world-famous non-stop express at King's Cross before the great event when I was shown photographs of the train with the corridor tender, and yet I made a mistake; perhaps it was perfectly natural, I leave you to judge.

The journey from Croydon to Northumberland was uneventful. We came down at Bircham Newton for fuel, but bumpy flying conditions over Lincolnshire and Yorkshire made us 20 minutes late on the ground at Cramlington. Here I was glad to receive a message thrown from the *Flying Scotsman* saying the train wireless had heard my signals to Croydon and expected to pick up conversation very clearly whilst crossing the Border. The message also said a flashlight had been arranged to signal from the fourth coach of the train, so that when

we took the air I had hopes of quickly flying alongside the non-stop at the appointed place, Berwick Border Bridge.

Conditions were not too kind, however, when we passed over Alnwick Castle about 4.35. Nearing Beal we sighted a long white streak of steam and on reaching this express I read quite clearly the signboards on the carriages indicating that the train was for Edinburgh. Speaking to the train I said that I would fly beside them across the bridge on the westward side and as our speed was much greater than the train I circled over the sea coming back to cross the Tweed just as the express reached the south end of the bridge. It was necessary to climb quickly after dipping almost to the level of the rails over the river, as we looked back over the town I was amazed to see the express stopping in the station. The absence of the pre-arranged flashing light signals also made me think that something was wrong with the train, or that the train was not the *Flying Scotsman*. A message from the saloon quickly confirmed the latter. "You have picked up the 'Junior Scotsman' which stops at Berwick, suggest you follow rail lines as far as Dunbar."

Our speed was then about 70 miles an hour, so I opened up and headed

Imperial Airways bi-plane, the 'City of Glasgow', flying over the River Tweed at Berwick. The locomotive pictured is in fact the 'Junior Scotsman', which the pilot had temporarily confused with the Flying Scotsman.

north with the indicator touching 100 m.p.h. Fifteen minutes later we were rewarded by the sight of another streak of white smoke, the real non-stop making for Edinburgh for all he was worth. At 5.20 p.m. I called him apologising for missing the train at Berwick and asking for a signal; this time responding flashes came from the fourth carriage. Again I apologised and explained that a heavy headwind had reduced our speed. Congratulating the train on its being ahead of time I swung over the speeding express and as time was running short turned for Edinburgh notched up all out, after asking the train not to push ahead too hard as the air party wished to be on the platform at Waverley to meet the train contingent as arranged. My last message was, "Hope you have had a

good journey, ours not too good owing to headwind, but everything O.K."

Touching 115 m.p.h. the plane reached Turnhouse Aerodrome at 5.45. We scrambled out into waiting motor cars and after a couple of traffic delays reached Waverley Station at 6.10 p.m. to find the train in the station and a cheery greeting from the railway party, and your Chief General Manager and General Manager for Scotland.

After very welcome hospitality I returned to King's Cross in an excellent sleeping berth, glad to think that the day had been a success. But I would suggest that you paint big white letters on the roof of your real non-stop *Flying Scotsman* to prevent further mistakes by airmen in the future.

RIGHT: Passengers ready to depart on the Flying Scotsman, Kings Cross circa 1934.

THE PERMANENT WAY
Comfort and Curves

(Taken from The London & North Eastern Railway Magazine *November 1928)*

The Permanent Way used to be the responsibility of The Engineer, the number one, a man whose responsibilities were enormous, for they included all Works and Bridges by way of a start. He was a professional Civil Engineer of the highest standing, as were his up-and-coming younger men.

The great British public generally desires to be carried on its railway journeys with speed and comfort, but there are exceptions as the following true incident illustrates:—

A year or two ago the guard of the *Flying Scotsman* while passing along the corridor was called by a lady to her compartment. "Is this really the *Flying Scotsman*'? she asked, "I thought it went very fast." "Yes, Madam, it is, and we are travelling over 60 miles an hour," he replied. "Oh," she ejaculated incredulously, "it doesn't seem like it. I came from Twinkleton to London this morning," she added, "and my word, we did travel fast; I was nearly thrown from one side of the carriage to the other." "Yes, Madam, and how long did it take you to make that journey?" courteously asked the guard. The lady supplied the time and the approximate distance. The guard then explained that as the average rate must have been less than 20 miles an hour, she could not have been going at anything like the speed at which she was then travelling. "Ah well," she sniffed, "it felt a lot faster, at any rate." You see, there are some people who like to *feel* that they are getting their money's worth all the time.

However, the L.N.E.R. tries to please the majority, and for this reason they have attached to their staff *"the most sensitive passenger in the world."*

This silent traveller is often to be seen, to the great curiosity of passengers and platform staff alike, riding on the floor of a reserved compartment, with two attendants. It is a weird-looking brass instrument (see photographs) [about] 2 ft. high and 1 ft. square, and has its "free pass" made out to the "Hallade Track Register."

It was invented by the late Mons. Hallade, a French railway engineer, and first introduced into England by Mr. Chas. J. Brown, the Chief Engineer of the Southern Area. It does not appear on the salary list, but performs important work better than the best-paid official could achieve.

To understand its duties you should, when tired of reading, try to analyse the motions of the carriage in which you are riding. If you separate them carefully in your mind you will find they are in three directions.

1st.—Forward and backward shocks to and from the direction in which the train is travelling. These are, of course, most noticeable in the starting and stopping of the trains.

2nd.—Sways from side to side of the coach.

3rd.—Upward bumps and jerks through the carriage springs.

Now this "most sensitive passenger" not only separates its own sensations into the three components referred to but writes as it runs exactly how much its feelings have been hurt, and where,

The Hallade track register.

and the depth of its feelings are shown by the length of the cross lines it draws.

Its mechanism is most ingenious. A drum of white paper is unrolled by clockwork at a constant speed and on this three uncanny fingers rest and write; but the remarkable peculiarity of the machine is shown by the fact that each of these fingers most religiously minds its own business. The finger which records the sways from side to side is quite unperturbed by any forward or backward motion of the coach, and vertical bumps leave it quite cold. The finger with the needle point which watches the up and down bumps of the coach is serenely unconscious of any other movement taking place; and lastly, the needle whose duty it is to record the backward and forward movements is in turn totally oblivious of any other motion.

This discrimination is due to a complicated arrangement of bars and balance weights which are to be seen at the back of the machine.

There is also, it must be explained, a modest little finger resting on the drum which is not interested in any vibrations at all. It is connected by an indiarubber tube to a bulb held in the hand of one of the attendants, who spends the time with his head (adorned by goggles over the eyes) hanging out of the window, noting the mile posts and stations, &c. As each quarter-mile post flashes past he presses the bulb once, and a small kick appears on the otherwise monotonous straight line traced on the moving paper by this little finger; at each mile-post two pressures and two marks show; at stations three marks are made.

The chief attendant with pencil in hand paternally hovers over the working machine the whole time writing the names of the stations and the figures of the mile-posts on the revolving drum of paper, as these are called out to him by the first attendant.

When the run is finished the resulting long strip of paper is taken away and spread out on the office desk. Here the "complaints" of each needle are now carefully examined and their origin decided. Their position is determined by the adjacent mile-posts, and the engineers responsible for the maintenance of the track are advised of their existence and instructed to remedy the causes.

Closely allied to the subject of comfort in riding is the serious question of adjusting exisiting curves on railways.

On an ideal railway the passenger should rise round all the curves that exist as comfortably as he does on a perfectly conditioned straight road; whether he was on a curve or not, but we all know that ideal has not yet been universally attained.

When the railways were first constructed nearly all curves were made to a perfectly regular radius, but the passage of time and the passage of trains have made sad havoc of that perfection, and unfortunately as the variations are not easily detected by the naked eye, costly obstructions such as bridges, signals, &c., have in many cases been erected close to these distortions, making it impossible to return the curves to their original regularity.

The causes of these distortions demand a look at one of the idiosyncracies of curves. To illustrate this feature take a bent sprint fixed at the ends; if by pressing your finger you flatten it at any point, it immediately retaliates by bulging out into two very much sharper curves on each side, and that, as a general rule is what has happened to the original railway curves. This action is easily understood when it is remembered that engines from the time they are built take a dislike to curves, and are always endeavouring to straighten them out, with the result that in time. "Natural" curves are converted into a series of "sharps" and "flats."

RIGHT: In the 1920s and 30s the L.N.E.R. press department worked extremely hard to nurture the image of the Flying Scotsman. This poster shows a silhouetted pair of hands shaking a cocktail shaker. The cocktail bar was one of many facilities passengers could take advantage of on their journey between London's King's Cross and Waverley Station, Edinburgh.

ON THE *FLYING SCOTSMAN*

By Eric Gill

(*Taken from* London & North Eastern Railway Magazine *January 1933*)

Mr Cecil Dandridge was appointed Advertising Manager at L.N.E.R. in 1928. He was responsible for commissioning Eric Gill to introduce the typeface Gill Sans, which was then used on all L.N.E.R.'s posters and publicity material. The extract below is an account by Eric Gill of his journey on the *Flying Scotsman*. The locomotive was No. 2582, an A3 named Sir Hugo.

"Well, did you get your ride on the Engine?"

"Rather!"

"What was it like?"

"Marvellous, simply marvellous – a jolly sight more marvellous than you'd expect and yet in some ways quite the opposite."

I got to King's Cross about 9.30 (wasn't going to risk being late) and, after a cup of tea and a sandwich, I ventured into the Guard's van of the train, at which the guard, looking very spruce, had just arrived with bag and flags and what not, and said: "I say, good morning, look here, it's like this; I've got this engine pass to Grantham."

"Oh, have you?" "Yes, and, I say, can I leave my bag in here till I come off the engine?" No objection to that, so I stepped back on to the platform and there I saw Mr. Sparke, the District Locomotive Superintendent and a friend of his. Mr. Sparke had very kindly come to introduce me to Mr. Young of Newcastle, the driver of the engine, and his friend kindly presented me with a nice clean swab to wipe my hands on from time to time. (Forgot all about it afterwards, but kept it as a memento!) The engine, No. 2582 of Newcastle, then backed in and I was introduced to Mr. Young – very grand and important and an object of curiosity to the group of enthusiasts on the platform (I mean me, not Mr. Young).

I was born beside the railway at Brighton, and I spent most of my childhood examining and drawing locomotives, and what surprised me now was, first, how little things had changed in fundamentals since I was a child 35 years ago and, second, how simple in idea the mechanism of steam engines still is. A detail that struck me immediately was that the throttle lever on the L.N.E.R. engine was worked by pulling it upwards towards you, whereas on the engines of my Brighton childhood it was worked by a lever at right angles to the axis of the boiler.

The remaining few minutes were spent in explanations of the brake apparatus, steam pressure required – the names of this and that and then someone called up from outside: 'right you are' and I gathered that it must be exactly 10.0. The engine was driven from the right hand side, so I was given the piano-stool or perch on the left side, with one foot on a pail (a quite ordinary household looking pail) and the other dangling. Up to this time the fireman had been doing various odd jobs about the place. He now shut (if you can call it shutting, for it only about half covered the gap) the iron door between engine and tender, and Mr. Young, having made a suitable response to the man outside who had shouted "right you are," pulled up the handle (both hands to the job and not too much at a time – a mouthful, so to say, for a start, to let her feel the weight) and, well, we simply started forward. It's as simple as that. I mean it *looks* as simple as that.

And, immediately, the fireman started shovelling coal. I shouted some apology to him for taking his seat. I could not hear his reply. It was probably to say that he had not time for seats. He shovelled in about 6 shovelsful; then, after a few seconds pause, another half dozen – a few seconds pause and then six or more shovels and so on practically without stopping the whole time. What strikes you about this, even more than the colossal labour of the thing and the great skill with which he distributes the coal in the fire and his unerring aim in throwing a pretty big shovelful of coal through a not very large opening, what strikes you is the extraordinary primitive nature of the job. You stand in a space about as big as a hearth-rug spread out longways to the fire and you take a shovelful of coal out of a hole at one end and throw it through a hole in the other end – spilling a bit every time. You go on doing this for hours. Your attention must be as great as your skill and strength. You must watch the pressure gauges and you must watch the state of the fire at the same time. And your only relaxations are when, on entering tunnels or passing stations, you give a tug at the whistle handle and when, on a signal from the driver, you let down the water scoop to take up water from the trough between the rails (which occurs every hundred miles or so). And talking of primitive things, look at the whistle handle! It is a round ring on the end of a wire (there is one on each side of the cab). It dangles down about a foot from the roof. When the train is travelling fast you have to make a bit of a grab for it as it is never in the same place for two seconds together. On receiving a nod of acquiescence from Mr. Young, I pulled the handle myself as we approached Peterborough, and again as we went, at reduced speed, through the station itself. (My first pull was but a timid little shriek, but my second was, it seemed to me, a long bold blast.)

But don't imagine I'm complaining or sneering about this primitiveness. It's

*Mr Eric Gill (left) painted and affixed with his own hands, the name-plate of the most re-
nowned train of its day, the 'Flying Scotsman'. On the right of the group is Mr C.G.G. Danbridge,
advertising manager of the London and North Eastern Railway, who initiated the reform.*

no more primitive or less venerable than sawing with a hand saw or ploughing
with a horse plough. I only think that it's surprising how these primitive mehtods
persist. Here we were on a an engine of the most powerful kind in the world, at-
tahed to one of the most of all travelling hotels — the string of coaches called The
Flying Scotsman — with its Cocktail Bar and Beauty Parlours, its dining saloons,
decorated in more or less credible imitiation of the salons of 18th century France, its
waiters and guards and attendants of all sorts, its ventilation and heating apparatus as efficient as those of the Strand Palace Hotel, and here we were carrying on
as if we were pulling a string of coal trucks.

Though the engine is well sprung, there is a feeling of hard contact on the rails
all the time – somthing like riding on an enormously heavy solid-tyred bicycle.
And that rhythmic tune which you hear when travelling by train, the rhythm of
the wheels as they over the joins in the metals (iddy UMty... iddy UMty... &c)
is entirely absent. There is a continuous iddyiddyiddy... there is no sensation of
travelling *in* a train—you are travelling *on* an engine. You are on top of an extremely heavy sort of cart horse which is discharging its terrific pent-up energy
by the innumerable outbursts of its breath.

In the 1930s, passengers on the Flying Scotsman *had over seven hours to enjoy the succession of meals and snacks on offer in the restaurant cars. Fine dining was the hallmark of the service.*

And continuously the fireman works, and continuously the driver, one hand on the throttle lever, the other ready near the brake handle (a handle no bigger than that of a bicycle and yet controlling power sufficient to pull up a train weighing 500 tons) keeps watch on the line ahead for a possible adverse signal. If the signals are down they go straight ahead, slowing down only for the sharper curves and the bigger railway junctions. You place absolute trust in the organisation of the line and you know practically every yard of it by sight. You dash roaring into the small black hole of a tunnel (the impression you get is that it's a marvel you don't miss it sometimes) and when you're in you can see nothing at all. Does that make you slow up? Not at all – not by a ½ m.p.h. The signal was down; there *can't* be anything in the way and it's the same at night. I came back on the engine from Grantham in the evening, simply to find out what they *can* see. You can see nothing but the signals – you know your whereabouts simply by memory. And as for the signals: it's surprising how little the green lights show up compared with the red. It seemed to me that they went more by the absence of a red light (in the expected place) than by the presence of a green one. You can see the red miles away but the green only when you're almost on it. And if it seemed a foolhardy proceeding to rush headlong into tunnels in the day time, how much more foolhardy did it seem at night to career along at 80 miles an hour in a black world with nothing to help you but your memory of the road and a lot of flickering lights – lights often almost obliterated by smoke and rain. And here's another primitive thing: You can generally see nothing at all through the glass windows of the cab at night because the reflections of the firelight make it impossible. To see the road, to see the signals, you must put your head out at the side – weather or no. The narrow glass screen prevents your eyes from being filled with smoke and cinders, but, well, it seems a garden of Eden sort of arrangement all the same.

And they don't even fill the tender with coal of the required size. Sometimes a big lump gets wedged into the opening and has to be slowly broken up with a pickaxe before it can be dislodged – what about that? Well, I call it jolly fine; but it's jolly rum too, when you think of all the electric gadgets and labour-saving contrivances which the modern housewife thinks herself a martyr if she don't get.

Up the long bank before Grantham – yes, and, you notice the ups and down when you're on the engine. They are both visible and hearable. You hear the engine's struggle (there's no 'changing down' when it starts 'labouring'). You feel it too, and, looking straight ahead, and not only sideways like the millionaire in the train behind, you will see the horizon of the bank before you. It *looks* like a hill. And when you run over the brow you *see* the run down and you hear and feel the engine's change of breath, you hear and feel more easy thrust of the pistons.

And, on the return journey, going down into London in the dark (on No. 2750, with Mr. Gutteridge and Mr. Rayner, a London engine and London men) with steam shut off and fire nearly out – just enough fire to get home with – we were pulled up by an adverse signal. Good that was too. Nothing visible in the blackness but the red lights over our heads. Silence – during which the fireman told me that Mr Guttridge had driven the King 28 times. Suddenly one of the red lights turned green – sort of magical.

"Right ho," said the fireman.

Then

and NOW

200
RESTAURANT CARS
ON
L·N·E·R TRAINS

LONDON AND NORTH EASTERN RAILWAY

ABOVE: Buffet car interior of the Flying Scotsman, *1938.*

A Record L.N.E.R. Run

On November 30 the 185.8 miles from King's Cross to Leeds were run in 151 min. 56 sec. down and 157 min. 17 sec. up by the 4-6-2 locomotive 'Flying Scotsman'

(Taken from The Railway Gazette *December 1934)*

Much attention has been attracted in recent years to the possibilities of diesel propulsion, chiefly as the result of the successful working in Germany of the Flying Hamburger railcar between Berlin and Hamburg, and investigations have been taking place as to the adaptability of such units to business needs in this country. A test run was made by the L.N.E.R. on Friday, November 30, as a demonstration of the maximum speeds reasonably possible with an ordinary steam locomotive hauling a load to give accommodation similar to that of a diesel-electric unit such as the Flying Hamburger. If comparisons be sought, it should be remembered that the Flying Hamburger has to make one intermediate slack on its journey, at Wittenberge, to 37 m.p.h., and also to run cautiously for the first 8 miles of its journey, from Berlin to Spandau West, where speed is limited to 50 m.p.h., and similarly to restrain speed to 65 m.p.h. for some miles into Hamburg. The route over which it runs, however, is practically flat, whereas the London and North Eastern main line is by comparison quite heavily graded, as a reference to the profile reproduced herewith will show. Several severe speed reductions have to be made, notably through Peterborough, Doncaster, and Wakefield, and minor slowings at Grantham and Retford (in the down direction), and at Lofthouse in both directions.

A provisional schedule of 165 min. for the 185.8 miles' journey, each way, was laid down for the test train of four coaches, consisting of dynamometer car, a corridor first of the latest type, a first class dining and kitchen car, and a composite brake. Had the leading coach been a composite brake like the rear coach, instead of the dynamometer car, the seating accommodation of the train would have been 156 places, with full restaurant car accommodation. The tare weight of the test load was thus 144¾ tons behind the tender, and inclusive of the officials who travelled in the train, and recording apparatus and stores carried, 147 tons

RIGHT: This 1932 poster depicts the L.N.E.R. and the Flying Scotsman *as the embodiment of speed and modernity, whilst having a sly dig at the Southern Railway's 'Little Boy' poster. For all its stylish accomplishment, this poster was not well received by the travelling public, and therefore not re-issued in 1933.*

in all. The engine provided was No. 4472, 'Flying Scotsman', of the Pacific type, with boiler working at 180 lb. per sq. in.; this engine is now 11 years old, and had already run 653,071 miles, of which 44,176 miles had been covered since the last repair. No special preparation for the trial had been made. A slight experimental alteration to the blast-pipe, with a view to permitting of freer exhaust, had been made, one of several similar modifications now in course of trial on the L.N.E.R. The driver was W. Sparshatt, and the fireman R. Webster, both of King's Cross shed. Mr. V. M. Barrington Ward, Superintendent, Western Section, Southern Area, L.N.E.R., travelled in charge of the train, and was accompanied by Mr. C. J. Brown, Engineer, Southern Area, Mr. J. Miller, Engineer, North Eastern Area, Mr. O. V. Bulleid, Assistant to the Chief Mechanical Engineer, and other officials. In addition to the dynamometer car records, a Hallade record was made in the rear coach. The weather was misty, but the fog which had prevailed during the earlier part of the week had cleared; there was practically no wind.

On leaving the terminus, round the curve from No. 11 platform, the engine slipped slightly, but afterwards got away very rapidly up the initial 1 in 107 grade, and by Wood Green was doing 71½ m.p.h. Up the 1 in 200 thence to Potter's Bar speed was steady at 67 – 68 m.p.h. throughout. The descent to the Lea Valley was somewhat hampered, however, by the brakes leaking on slightly between Hatfield and Welwyn Garden City, bringing speed down from 83½ m.p.h. (before Hatfield) to 60 m.p.h. at m.p. 20, whence there was a recovery to 68½ m.p.h. up the 1 in 200 to Woolmer Green summit. Over the favourable stretch north of Stevenage very high speeds ruled; the average over the 24.1 miles from Hitchin to Offord was 90.2 m.p.h., with a maximum of 94.7 m.p.h. near Three Counties. Speed was well maintained at about the 90 m.p.h. level over the flat section past Biggleswade, Sandy, and Tempsford; and would have been continued as far as Huntingdon had not the engine been eased round the curves near Offord. Peterborough was thus passed in 39 sec. over the hour, a distance of 76.4 miles.

The most impressive section of the journey was that which immediately followed. Accelerating on the level to 80 m.p.h. at Tallington, the engine never dropped below that figure during the whole of the ascent to Stoke Summit. The 1 in 200 length was surmounted at a steady speed of 82.2 m.p.h., and after a momentary rise to 84 on the short and easier length through Corby station, the final three miles at 1 in 178 were surmounted with no lower minimum than 81

RIGHT: Driver W. Sparshatt, and his fireman, R. Webster on the day of the record run, at Kings Cross.

L.N.E.R. EXPERIMENTAL RUNS, LONDON TO LEEDS AND BACK. November 30, 1934
Engine, 4-6-2 No. 4472, 'Flying Scotsman'. Driver W. Sparshatt, Fireman Webster

DOWN JOURNEY
4 coaches, 144¾ t. tare, 147 t. gross

UP JOURNEY
6 coaches, 205¼ t. tare, 207½ t. gross

Distance	Schedule	Actual Times		**Max and Min Speeds	Stations	Distance	Schedule	Actual Times		**Max. and Min. Speeds
Miles	Min.	Min.	Sec.	M.p.h.		Miles	Min.	Min.	Sec.	M.p.h.
0.0	0	0	00	—	KING'S CROSS	185.8	165	157	17	—
2.5	—	4	04	55	FINSBURY PARK	183.3	—	153	22	—
3.4	—	4	59	—	Harringay	182.4	—	152	28	—
4.0	—	5	34	—	Hornsey	181.8	—	151	58	—
5.0	—	6	25	71½	Wood Green	180.8	—	151	13	81
6.4	—	7	40	67	New Southgate	179.4	—	150	09	83¾
9.2	—	10	07	68½	New Barnet	176.6	—	148	08	79¾
10.6	—	11	22	68	Hadley Wood	175.2	—	147	03	77½
12.7	—	13	16	67	Potter's Bar	173.1	—	145	16	69¾
14.6	—	14	41	—	Brookman's Park	171.2	—	143	47	72¼
17.7	19	17	03	83¼	HATFIELD	168.1	148	141	11	85
20.3	—	19	09	60‡	Welwyn Garden City	165.5	—	139	16	80
22.0	—	20	45	—	Welwyn North	163.8	—	137	58	77
23.5	—	22	06	68½	*Woolmer Green*	162.3	—	136	48	72
25.0	—	23	26	81¾†	Knebworth	160.8	—	135	31	76¼†
28.6	—	26	05	80¼	Stevenage	157.2	—	132	37	70¼
31.9	30	28	22	93½	HITCHIN	153.9	137	129	50	72½
35.7	—	30	48	94¾	Three Counties	150.1	—	126	43	76¼
37.0	—	31	40	85¾††	Arlesey	148.8	—	125	38	75
41.1	—	34	27	91¾	Biggleswade	144.7	—	122	00	62¼
44.1	—	36	24	92¾	Sandy	141.7	—	118	33	40‖
47.5	—	38	38	93¼	Tempsford	138.3	—	115	55	80¾
51.7	—	41	29	85	St. Neot's	134.1	—	112	38	71½
56.0	—	44	24	90§	Offord	129.8	—	109	08	eased
58.9	50	46	31	81¾	HUNTINGDON	126.9	116	106	42	80½
62.0	—	48	58	72½	*Mile-post 62*	123.8	—	104	13	—
63.5	—	50	11	—	Abbots Ripton	122.3	—	102	57	72
69.4	—	54	28	83¼	Holme	116.4	—	98	31	83¼
72.6	—	56	57	75	Yaxley	113.2	—	96	05	72½
75.0	—	58	57	—	*Fletton Junction*	110.8	—	93	52	—
76.4	66	60	39	21¶	PETERBOROUGH	109.4	100	92	00	25¶
78.0	—	63	29	—	*Mile-post 78*	107.8	—	90	10	—
79.5	—	64	20	71½	Werrington Junction	106.3	—	89	00	80¼
81.9	—	66	14	79	Helpston	103.9	—	87	14	84
84.8	—	68	26	80¼	Tallington	101.0	—	85	10	86½
88.6	—	71	13	84	ESSENDINE	97.2	—	82	38	98
92.2	—	73	47	83¾	Little Bytham	93.6	—	80	25	95½
97.1	—	77	21	82¼	Corby	88.7	—	77	11	85¾

Distance	Schedule	Actual Times		**Max and Min Speeds	Stations	Distance	Schedule	Actual Times		**Max. and Min. Speeds
100.1	—	79	33	81¼	Stoke	85.7	—	74	54	68½
102.0	—	80	58	87¼*	Great Ponton	83.8	—	73	14	68½
105.5	92	83	39	62¶	GRANTHAM	80.3	74	70	18	73¾
109.7	—	87	16	—	Barkstone	76.1	—	66	45	69‡‡
111.5	—	88	41	77½	Hougham	74.3	—	65	13	75
115.4	—	91	24	90	Claypole	70.4	—	62	13	78
120.1	103	94	38	86½	NEWARK	65.7	62	58	28	77½
126.4	—	99	10	82½	Carlton	59.4	—	53	44	—
127.4	—	99	54	81	Crow Park	58.4	—	53	01	81¾
131.3	—	102	56	—	Dukeries Junction	54.5	—	50	08	81¾
131.9	—	103	29	—	Tuxford	53.9	—	49	42	81¾
133.7	—	104	53	76½	Markham	52.1	—	48	23	73¾
135.5	—	—		83¾	Gamston	50.3	—	46	55	73¾
138.6	119	108	44	69¶	RETFORD	47.2	47	44	28	81½
141.7	—	111	19	81¾	Sutton	44.1	—	42	14	85
143.9	—	112	53	87	Ranskill	41.9	—	40	41	86½
145.8	—	114	11	88¼	Scrooby	40.0	—	39	23	88¼
147.7	—	115	30	—	Bawtry	38.1	—	38	04	83¾
149.5	—	116	50	79	Piper's Wood	36.3	—	36	44	73
151.3	—	118	08	87¼	Rossington	34.5	—	35	18	77½
153.2	—	119	31	—	Black Carr Junction	32.6	—	33	49	75
156.0	133	122	27	40¶	DONCASTER	29.8	32	30	58	35¶
158.8	—	124	29	—	Castle Hills	27.0	—	28	58	—
160.0	—	126	38	76¼	Carcroft	25.8	—	27	01	72¶
162.5	—	128	37	81¾	Hampole	23.3	—	25	03	81¾
164.7	—	130	17	80¼	South Elmsall	21.1	—	23	25	77½
—	—	—	77½							
167.9	—	132	41	81	Hemsworth	17.9	—	20	47	74½
170.4	—	134	37	77½	Nostell	15.4	—	18	33	61½
171.9	—	135	43	83¼	Hare Park	13.9	—	17	05	64½
174.2	—	137	26	—	Sandal	11.6	—	14	55	63¼
175.9	151	139	28	35¶	WAKEFIELD	9.9	14	12	42	39¶
177.0	—	—	57		Wrenthorpe North	8.8	—	11	16	—
178.3	—	141	22	40¶	Lofthouse	7.5	—	9	46	48¶
180.2	157	144	39	55½	Ardsley	5.6	9	7	46	54
183.3	—	147	46	68	Beeston	2.5	—	4	17	56
185.3	—	150	15	10¶	Holbeck	0.5	—	1	36	—
185.8	165	151	56	—	LEEDS (CENTRAL)	0.0	0	0	00	—

Down journey: Left King's Cross 9.8 a.m. Arrived Leeds (Central) 11.40 a.m.
Up journey: Left Leeds (Central) 2.0 p.m. Arrived King's Cross 4:37 p.m.
¶ Service slack; * Maximum before shutting off steam; † Maximum at Langley; ‡ Minimum by brakes leaking on from Hatfield to mile-post 20; § Maximum before easing for curves; †† Minimum at Langford; II Permanent-way relaying slack; ‡‡ Minimum at Peascliffe tunnel.
** At or at changes of gradient near station shown in centre column.

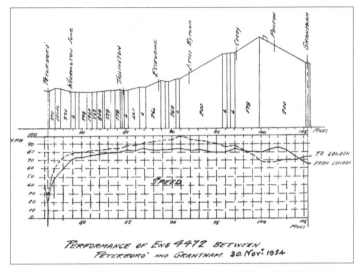

Performance of Eng. 4472 between Peterboro' and Grantham, 30 November 1934.

m.p.h., where the engine was working at 40 per cent. cut-off. The ten miles between posts 90 and 100 occupied 7 min. 16.4 sec., which gives an average speed of
82.5 m.p.h. throughout. Speed was eased below Great Ponton, and reduced to
62 m.p.h. through Grantham, also to 69 m.p.h. through Retford. The highest
speeds attained here were 90 m.p.h. near Claypole and 88¼ m.p.h. at Scrooby. In
the first two hours from King's Cross, including the severe slack through Peterborough, the train travelled 153¾ miles, so averaging 76.9 m.p.h. to this point; the
150 miles from Harringay to Black Carr Junction, pass to pass, were covered at an
average of 78.4 m.p.h.

After slowing to 40 m.p.h. for the divergence north of Doncaster, and further
slight trouble with brakes leaking on from there to Castle Hills, the engine attained 81¾ m.p.h. up the 1 in 440 to Hampole, and surmounted both the 1½-mile
stretches at 1 in 150 that follow without the speed falling below 77½ m.p.h. More
remarkable, perhaps, was the recovery from the 35 m.p.h. slowing through Wakefield to 57 m.p.h. up the succeeding 1 in 100, and speed was still rising when it
had to be reduced for Lofthouse curve. After passing Holbeck at a dead slow
speed, the train stopped at Leeds Central station in 151 min. 56 sec. from London, having thus achieved a start-to-stop average of 73.4 m.p.h., and cut just over
13 min. from the provisional schedule. Out of this distance a total of no less

L.N.E.R. employees measuring brake horse power in the Dyanometer car attached to the Flying Scotsman, *in April 1931.*

than 155 miles had been covered at an average of 80 m.p.h. For the return journey, as previously mentioned, the load was made up to six vehicles, weighing empty 205¼ tons, and 207½ tons in all behind the engine tender. The sharp rise for ⅜-mile from Holbeck at 1 in 50 was surmounted at 36½ m.p.h., and 56 attained before the commencement of the 3¼ miles at 1 in 100 to Ardsley, which were mounted steadily at 54 m.p.h. On the succeeding descent speed barely exceeded 60 m.p.h., and severe slacks were necessary at Lofthouse and Wakefield. Also, after mounting the 1 in 150 to Nostell at 61½ m.p.h. minimum, slight speed reductions at both Hemsworth and beyond Hampole had to be made on the falling grades to Doncaster. After slowing to 35 m.p.h. at Doncaster, the engine performed a striking feat of acceleration. Assisted by ¾-mile falling at 1 in 264, and followed by level track for 2¾ miles, speed rose in 4 miles from the slack to 77½ m.p.h., did not fall below 73 m.p.h. up 2½ miles at 1 in 198 to Piper's Wood, and rose again to 88¼ down the similarly-inclined 3-mile descent to Scrooby troughs. Nothing further of exceptional note occurred until the long ascent of 14 miles to Stoke summit had been surmounted at a minimum speed of 68½ m.p.h. Speed steadily rose down the succeeding bank, until a culmination was reached with an average rate of 97.3 m.p.h. over the 3 m. 46½ c. from Little Bytham to Essendine. The observers

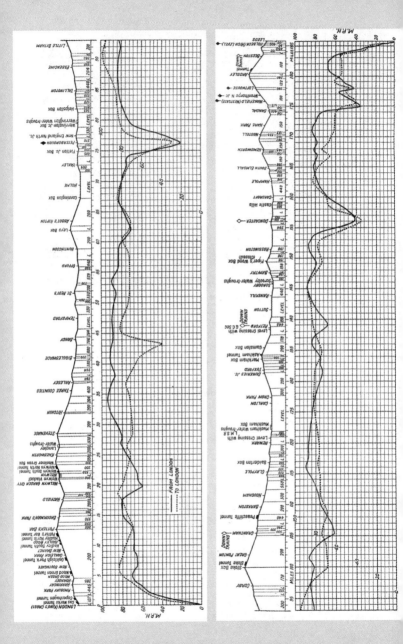

in the train, timing by means of stop-watches, from the mile posts, made the maximum speed achieved vary from 98 to 100 m.p.h. This difference represents only ⅕ sec. over a ¼ mile, and as the dynamometer record showed 100 m.p.h., there is no reason to dispute this figure.* The 15.2 miles from Corby to Helpston were run at an average of 90.2 m.p.h.

Beyond Peterborough the running was, for the most part, of slightly less note; 8 min. had been gained on the provisional schedule to this point, but over one or two subsequent stages, the engine, after the sustained and arduous power output of this lengthy journey, began to show symptoms of slight shortness of steam, notably at Huntingdon. The fireman must, indeed, have been feeling the strain involved in shifting a total of 9 tons of coal on the round journey. A permanent way check was also encountered at Sandy, causing a probable loss of slightly under 2 min. Nevertheless, the long ascent to Stevenage was surmounted at a minimum speed of 71 m.p.h. – another excellent achievement – and with comparatively moderate speed down the final descent from Potter's Bar, King's Cross was reached in 157 min. 17 sec. from Leeds, or 155½ min. net. Thus the journey was completed at an average start-to-stop speed of 70.9 m.p.h., and in 7¾ min. less than the provisional schedule, or 9½ min. less, if allowance be made for the Sandy check. Of the up journey a total of 94½ miles was run at an average of 80 m.p.h., making, with the down journey, a total of exactly 250 miles of the round trip covered at this high speed. Between 35 and 40 miles were traversed at the higher average of 90 m.p.h. Both these runs were faster from start-to-stop than any runs of such length previously made in Great Britain, and from the records available it is safe to say that no steam locomotive in any part of the world has previously achieved such a feat as to cover 250 miles in the course of one round trip at so high an average speed as eighty miles an hour. The times and speeds on the journey, as tabulated in this description, were recorded by Mr. Cecil J. Allen, M.inst.T., who also broadcast an eye-witness account of the journey in the National programme on the same evening.

* We reproduce the official L.N.E.R. graph of this part of the run.

LEFT: *Gradient profile of the Kings Cross–Leeds L.N.E.R. main line over which the remarkable test runs of November 30 were made at speeds shown by two graphs. Severe speed restrictions shown by black diamonds, slight restrictions by white diamonds.*

WORKING TRAFFIC OF A DOUBLE LINE OVER A SINGLE LINE OF RAILS DURING REPAIRS OR OBSTRUCTION.

(Taken from London & North Eastern Railway Rule Book 1933*)*

On the route of the *Flying Scotsman* (London to Aberdeen) there was only one stretch of single line track. This was north of Dundee and was between Usan and Montrose South signal boxes in order to cross a narrow iron viaduct spanning the risk Esk.

The following extract describes the rules that have to be put in place when running from double line to single line traffic.

189. When the traffic of a double line has to be worked over a single line of rails during repairs or owing to an obstruction, the following precautions must be adopted.

190. Single line working should be confined to the shortest length practicable and, whenever possible, between crossover roads where there are fixed signals, but in the event of a crossover road not protected by fixed signals being used the provisions of Rule 199 must be observed.

191. A competent person must be appointed as Pilotman, who must wear round his left arm above the elbow, a red armlet with the word "Pilotman" shown thereon in white letters, thus:–

If this armlet is not immediately available the Pilotman must wear a red flag in the position indicated until the proper armlet is obtained.

192. Except as provided in Rule 200, clause *(f)*, and in the first paragraph of Rule

LEFT: Poster produced by L.N.E.R. to advertise the excellent service passengers can expect from waiters in the dining restaurant carriages.

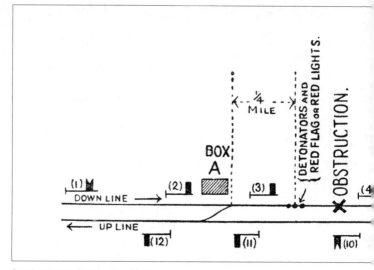

Signals to kept at Danger—Nos. 3, 5, 8.

Signals to be kept at Caution—Nos. 1, 4, 7.

Signals to be worked, where possible—Nos. 2, 6, 9, 10, 11, 12.

NOTE.—No 2 must be kept at Danger where No. 3 is not provided.

Signal No. 4 to be fogged on wrong line during fog or falling snow.

NOTE.—On the Great Western Railway 2 detonators are used at distant signal (No. 7).

206, no train must be allowed to enter upon or foul any portion of the single line without the Pilotman being present and riding upon the engine, except when a train is to be followed by one or more trains in the same direction, in which case the Pilotman must personally order each train to proceed and must ride upon the engine of the last train. When an engine supplied specially for the use of the Pilotman is coupled to a train it must be attached to the front unless it is necessary for such engine to be used for banking purposes where the use of bank engines is authorised. If the Pilotman travels on a train with two or more engines he must ride upon the rearmost engine. If the Pilotman travels on an electric train, rail motor or motor train he must ride with the Driver.

The Pilotman must show himself on each occasion to the Signalman at each box he passes, to the Handsignalman at catch and other points and to Fogsignalmen when on duty.

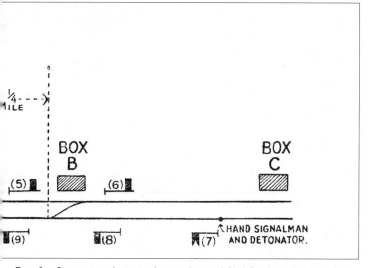

Box A.—*Down trains to be accepted in accordance with Block Regulation 4 or 5 (see Rule 200, clause (b)), and Up trains under Blcok Regulation 4,5 or 25 (a/iii) (see Rule 200, clauses (b) and (e)).*

Box B.—*Down trains to be accepted under Block Regulation 4 or 25 (a/iii) and Up trains under Block Regulations 5 (see Rule 200, clause (a)), or Block Regulations 4 (see Rule 200, clause (c)).*

193. (*a*) The Station Masters or other responsible persons at both ends of the obstructed section must communicate with each other by the most expeditious means, agree as to who shall arrange for pilot-working, and have a clear understanding as to the arrangements to be put into operation.

(*b*) It will generally be found more expeditious for the Station Master or other responsible person in advance of the obstruction to undertake the arrangements, as the Pilotman with the single line forms can then make his first journey by train or trolley, if either is available, on the proper running line. Under no circumstances must a train or trolley be allowed to run over the unobstructed line *in the wrong direction* until the Pilotman's form is signed by the Signalman at each end of the single line section, and also at any intermediate signal box.

(*c*) The person arranging single line working must fill up, sign, and address single line forms (*see* page 189 for specimen form) to—

(i.) The Signalmen controlling the crossover roads between which sin gle line working is to be put in operation.

(ii.) The Signalman at any signal box and the Station Master at any station that is intermediate on the line which is to be worked as a single line, provided such signal box or station is open or likely to be open during the time single line working is in operation.

(iii.) The person who will act as Pilotman.

(iv.) The Station Master at each end of the single line, except where the signal box at which single line working commences or finishes is not at a station and the ordinary working at the station will not be interfered with.

These forms must be handed to the Pilotman who must also sign all the forms issued and deliver the necessary form to the Signalman in charge of the crossover road at which the single line working commences and then proceed to the other end of the section. The Pilotman on his way must verbally inform persons in charge of level crossings, Gangers, Lengthaner and any other men at work on the line, that single line working is about to be commenced and which line will be used; he must also leave the necessary form with the person in charge of any intermediate signal box or station then open. On his arrival at the other end of the single line section the Pilotman must deliver the necessary forms to the Station Master and Signalman. Each person when receiving the form must sign the Pilotman's form. Trains may then be allowed to pass over the single line by the permission and under the control of the Pilotman.

Where the crossover road at each end of the line to be worked as a single line is under the control of one Signalman, these instructions must be observed, except that the single line form will be issued to the Signalman concerned.

When a Station Master himself acts as Pilotman he must retain only the Pilotman's form, and unless his station comes within the exception mentioned in section (iv.) of this clause (*c*), he must address and give a form to the person he leaves in charge of his station.

Should any intermediate signal boxes or stations be opened after single line working has commenced, the Pilotman must, as soon as practicable, advise the persons in charge of such places that single line working is in operation. He must also hand forms signed by the person who arranged the single line working and himself, to the Signalman and Station Masters concerned, who must sign the form held by the Pilotman.

(*d*) Station Masters and persons in charge issuing and receiving single line forms will be responsible for the Inspectors, Signalmen, and others concerned

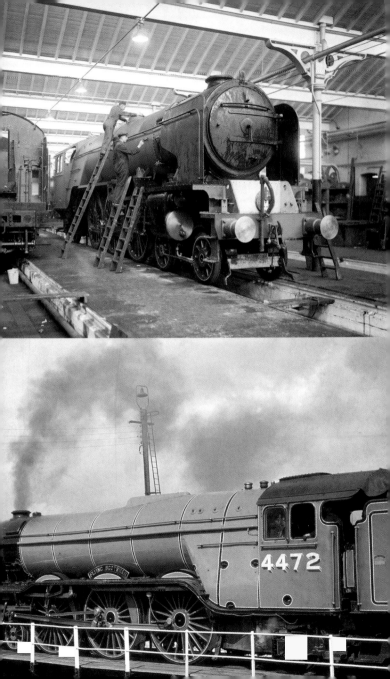

at their station being made acquainted with the circumstances immediately, and instructed in their necessary duties.

Twelve single line forms must be kept in a convenient place at each station, and at every signal box where there is a crossover road, so as to be available at any time.

194. (*a*) At each end of the obstructed line 3 detonators must be placed on such line 10 yards apart, ¼ mile, or more if necessary, from the point where single line working commences (see diagram on pages 62 and 63). When, however, the distance from the obstruction to the point where single line working commences is less then ¼ mile, the detonators must be placed as far from the obstruction as circumstances permit.

(*b*) A red flag by day, and a red light after sunset or during fog or falling snow must also be placed on the obstructed line near to the detonators. When lights are used these must show a Danger signal towards both the obstruction and the crossover road.

(c) During fog or falling snow a Fogsignalman must, whenever possible, be provided at the distant signal for the obstructed line operated from the box at which the trains are crossed to their proper line and he must place a detonator for each train travelling in the wrong direction on the line which is being used as a single line, opposite the distant signal and exhibit a hand Caution signal, in order that Drivers approaching the facing crossover road may be advised of their position. The Pilotman must instruct the Fogsignalman accordingly. Until a Fogsignalman is stationed at this signal the Pilotman must specially warn all Drivers that the Fogsignalman has not taken up duty.

If a fog or snowstorm occurs when single line working is in operation, the Signalman must, when this Fogsignalman commences duty, inform him of the single line working, and instruct him to act in accordance with the preceding paragraph. The Signalman at any intermediate signal box must instruct the Fogsignalmen, where employed, to place the detonators on the line being used as a single line for trains running in the direction to which the signal applies.

   NOTE.— On the Great Western Railway 2 detonators, 10 yards apart, are used at the distant signal referred to in clause (c).

195. (*a*) All points, including spring points and unworked trailing points, which become facing points to trains running over the single line, must be secured so as to ensure trains passing safely over them. In the case of spring points and unworked trailing points, the person instituting the single line working must arrange for a competent man to be appointed to hand-signal trains over them.

A relief fireman and driver await their turn for driving duties circa 1930. With the introduction of the corridor tender this meant that the Flying Scotsman *did not have to stop to change drivers and firemen.*

(*b*) The person instituting the single line working must arrange for all catch points in the single line to be closed and firmly secured before single line working is commenced. He must also arrange for a man, provided with hand signals and detonators, to be placed at such points with instructions to see that they are continuously kept closed and secured during the whole of the time that single line working is in operation.

196. (*a*) When a train is approaching catch points, spring points or unworked trailing points in the facing direction, the man at the points must, provided they are right for the train to pass over them, give the Driver a green hand signal held steadily.

(*b*) The Pilotman must satisfy himself that the Driver is aware of the location of these points, and Drivers must not pass over any of them in the facing direction until they have received a signal to do so from the man at the points.

RIGHT: The 'Flying Scotsman' departs from King's Cross in July 1933.

WALSCHAERT'S VALVE GEAR

(Inside Admission)

(Taken from London & North Eastern Railway
The Locomotiveman's Pocket Book 1947)

Walschaert was a young Belgian engineer and his valve-gear dated back to 1844 but it was not until the 1920s that it became virtually universal on our larger engines. Its advantages were adaptability, accessibility, suitability for short-cut-off working and reduction or elimination of moving parts such as eccentrics.

With this gear the motion of the valve is obtained from a combination of levers, one movement being worked from the crosshead and the other from the eccentric rod attached to the driving crank. The first named gives the lap and lead motion; the latter gives the additional travel necessary to the valve. Diagram No. 13 shows fully all the levers with the names indicating such and each man must become thoroughly conversant with the work done by each part. One important feature of this gear is that it gives the same lead opening in all positions of the reserving lever, this being made possible by the distance between the points where the radius rod and the valve spindle are coupled to the combination lever.

TWO-CYLINDER ENGINES

Question 117—Name the different parts of the Walschaert valve gear.

Answer–   Eccentric crank.

           Eccentric rod.

           Radius rod.

           Radius link.

           Crosshead arm.

           Union link.

           Combination lever.

           Valve spindle link *three-cylinder engines only.*

           Equal lever *three-cylinder engines only.*

           Two to one lever *three-cylinder engines only.*

           Reversing slide block.

           Die block.

Question 118 – How would you treat a broken eccentric crank, eccentric rod or foot of radius link?

Answer – Take down broken parts and disconnect reversing arm or link from the

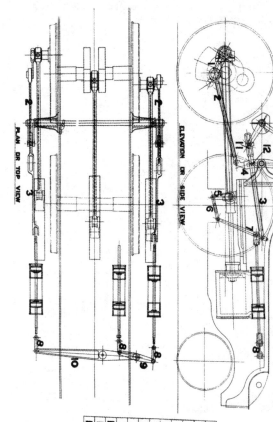

PLAN OR TOP VIEW

ELEVATION OR SIDE VIEW

1	ECCENTRIC CRANK
2	ECCENTRIC ROD
3	RADIUS ROD
4	RADIUS LINK
5	CROSSHEAD ARM
6	UNION LINK
7	COMBINATION LEVER
8	VALVE SPINDLE LINK
9	EQUAL LEVER
10	2 TO 1 LEVER
11	REVERSING SLIDEBLOCK
12	DIEBLOCK

PROGRESSIVE METHOD OF TESTING VALVES AND PISTONS ON 3 CLYLINDER ENGINES (INSIDE ADMISSION) DIAGRAM No. 22

STAGE 1
Testing R.B. Valve Head

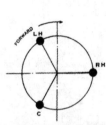

Set R.H. Crank on front centre i.e. in line with Connecting Rod.

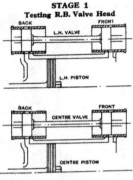

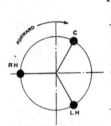

Set R.H. Crank on back centre i.e. in line with Connecting Rod.

With lever in mid-gear and Cylinder Cocks open, the only steam issuing should be from the right front Cylinder Cock as the right hand front Port will be open to lead.

Note—When testing Valves the Cylinder Cokcs are open, but when testing Pistons the Cylinder Cocks are closed, and a blow at the Chimney indicates defective Piston.
Live Steam being admitted to the Cyldiner is shewn by a **Red Line**. Steam passing a defective Piston Head and into the Exhaust Passages, Blast Pipe and Chimney is shewn by a **Dotted Line**.

radius rod. Place the die block in the centre of radius link and pack with wood top and bottom. See that the cylinder is lubricated, and proceed without any further disconnections.

Question 119 – How would you treat a broken radius rod, radius link other than foot or seized die block?

Answer – In each case take off the eccentric rod, disconnect reversing arm or link and take out union link, place the valve central and secure, but after centring the valve, the bottom of combination lever must be moved forward or gud-

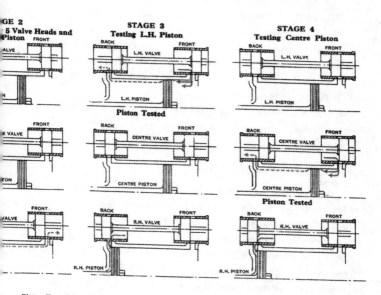

STAGE 2
5 Valve Heads and Piston

STAGE 3
Testing L.H. Piston

Piston Tested

STAGE 4
Testing Centre Piston

Piston Tested

Piston Tested (Lead Steam)

With lever in mid-gear and Cylinder Cocks open, the right hand back Port is open to lead. All other Ports are closed to steam. The only steam issuing should be from the right back Cylinder Cock.

With Lever in mid-gear and Cylinder Cocks closed, the R.H. Piston is tested.

With lever in 40% forward gear and Cylinder Cocks closed, the L.H. Piston is tested.

With lever in 40% backward gear and Cylinder Cocks closed, the Centre Piston is tested.

geon pin will strike it if allowed to hang straight down.

Question 120 – How would you treat a broken crosshead arm, union link or combination lever?

Answer – In the case of a broken crosshead arm or union link, take off the broken parts and eccentric rod. Disconnect reversing link from radius rod, place the die block in the centre of radius link and pack with wood top and bottom, place the valve central and secure, moving combination lever as in Answer 119–If combination lever is broken below the level of the gudgeon pin treat as above, but if the combination lever is broken above the level of the gudgeon pin there is no need to do anything, but take off the union link, and in this case there is even no need to centre the valve for on starting the radius rod will move the valve until it reaches its central position, and it will then remain stationary; also there is no need to be particular about the position of the gear at the next stop, because if the good side is then on a centre the stub of the combination lever can be moved to open whichever port is required on that side to cause the engine to move again.

Question 121 – State what you would do to clear Main Line immediately.

Answer – If broken parts were safe I would proceed clear of Main Line without disconnecting.

THREE-CYLINDER ENGINES

On engines fitted with three cylinders the methods of dealing with defective parts are the same as those enumerated for the two-cylindered engines.

The middle valve, however, is so arranged that it is operated from the motion of the two outside valves through rocking levers, known as the "two to one" and "equal" levers. When any of the gear working the outside valve is defective special methods have to be arranged to deal with the middle valve, which becomes inoperative. Nos. 8, 9 and 10 on diagram are the levers which are concerned.

Question 122 – In the event of either of the outside valves or gear becoming defective, other than those parts enumerated in Question No. 118, how would you treat the middle valve?

Answer – Take down the outside spindle link (No. 8 on the diagram) opposite to the failure, place the middle valve, and the valve on the defective side central and secure them; this will allow of one outside engine being worked. See that the centre piston and the outside piston on defective side are lubricated; work engine to nearest depot.

Question 123 – What would you do in the event of a defect occurring to the middle engine which necessitated the middle valve being closed?

Answer – Take down the two outside valve spindle links (No. 8 on the diagram), place the middle valve central and secure. This would allow both outside engines to be worked. See that the centre piston is well lubricated.

THREE-CYLINDER SIMPLE ENGINE

It is necessary that some explanation should be given with regard to the position of the cranks on the shaft.

The cranks for three-cylinder engines whose cylinder centre lines are in the same plane, are placed on the shaft at an equal distance from each other of 120°. This is clearly shown on Diagram No. 8 [not shown here]. When the middle cylinder is inclined at an angle different from that of the outside cylinders, in order that the centre connecting rod shall clear the leading axle, as in the case of Pacific and K.3 class engines, etc. the cranks are not equally spaced at 120° but vary slightly according to the difference in the angle of inclination.

Diagram No. 22 shows the relative positions of the cranks of the typical 3-cylinder engine, in the first case with the right hand crank on the front centre and the corresponding positions of the valves and pistons with the lever in mid gear, and in the second case with the right hand crank on back centre and the corresponding positions of the valves and pistons with the lever in mid gear, 40 per centre. forward gear and 40 per cent. backward gear.

A method of testing valves and pistons is shown on this diagram.

The following is a further method of testing pistons and valves —

To test for a piston blow, test each engine separately and make use of the cylinder cocks to indicate which piston is defective.

The best position to set the engine is when the piston is about 6 in. on its forward stroke. The lever is then put into fore gear and a blow from both cylinder cocks indicates that the rings are defective.

To test for a valve blow, take each valve in turn, setting its crank on the top or bottom quarter, with the lever in mid-gear. If the valves are in order, there will be no blow from any cylinder cock.

If a defect in the inside steam rings or valve heads is suspected and is not revealed by the test shown on Diagram 22, the alternative test as shown above should be made.

SIGNALS

(Taken from The Flying Scotsman *by Alan Anderson 1949)*

Alan Anderson wrote a series of railway books about famous train services. In this extract he explains the purpose and importance of signals.

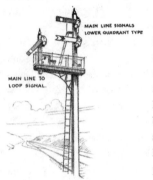

MAIN LINE SIGNALS
LOWER QUADRANT TYPE

MAIN LINE TO
LOOP SIGNAL.

Although Hitchin is only some 30 miles from London we have already passed a considerable number of signals. The driver of our locomotive will be watching the signals first and foremost throughout his run, for they will tell him not only whether he is to continue or stop, but will acquaint him with the state of the line for two or three sections ahead and from these he knows if he can go "all out" or if he is to proceed at a reduced speed.

Whilst colour light signalling is gradually

ELECTRIC
BANNER SIGNAL

replacing the semaphore type there are still considerable stretches of line controlled by the latter, and on some of the earlier parts of our route we may also catch sight of one of the old "Somersault" type – a reminder of the Great Northern days. We shall see colour light signals with three and four aspects, the order of the three aspect light

GROUND POSITION LIGHT
SHUNTING SIGNAL

being (from bottom to top) red, orange, green; on a four aspect light we have red, orange, green, orange. The red, of course, means 'stop'; one orange indicates that the section immediately ahead is clear but warns the driver of a possible 'stop' farther on. Two orange lights indicate that two sections ahead are clear whilst green means that three or more sections are clear.

SEARCHLIGHT
SIGNAL GIVING
4 ASPECTS.

A row of small white lights inclined above the signal lights, when lit, indicate that the train is to be diverted left or right according to the direction in which the lights point. These take the place of the low loop line arm on the semaphore type of signals.

WELWYN VIADUCT

3-ASPECT COLOUR LIGHT SIGNAL WITH DIVERSION INDICATOR ABOVE

When we reach York we shall enter a stretch of line which is under the control of one of the most modern systems of colour light signalling. Searchlight signals having one lens only are also in use and normally do not show any light. As a train is approaching, the signalman sets his signal levers to give the train the right of way, and the train itself causes the signal to light up with a very powerful searchlight showing orange or green which changes to red as the engine passes, and stays red until the train has entered the next section. Where two searchlight signals are mounted on one post four aspects can be shown including the two orange lights as referred to previously.

Unfortunately, it is not the privilege of every traveller to visit the train control room in charge of each section, but if we could see inside we should realise to what a high pitch train control has reached. Train control from a central point

4-ASPECT COLOUR LIGHT SIGNAL

was introduced into this country generally about 10 years ago, its object being to plot on track diagrams the passage of all trains and light engines in the area, and it has contributed largely to train running efficiency. In the control room are experienced men operators, one to each section of track, each with headphones on, and a diagram of the track in front of him. As our train passes specified reporting points, word is sent immediately to the train control room and the operator at once moves a card representing and describing our train on his diagram, so that he has the position and time of the train marked at each given point with only a few minutes' delay. At Darlington, for instance, there are ten men doing this work constantly in each eight hour shift, three shifts per day for every day of the year. Why do the railways go to all this trouble? The object is to see possible sources of delay which would not be apparent otherwise, and the operators are able to instruct signalmen how to act in order to keep the trains running smoothly. In the event of bad weather conditions when trains are delayed the control room plays a most important part in keeping the delays to a minimum. On this journey our train will come under the control of no less than four district control rooms between Doncaster and Berwick alone.

Alan Pegler interviewed by Hugh Gould

20 September 2000

Alan Pegler bought the 'Flying Scotsman' in 1962 for £3,000 from British Rail and under his ownership the locomotive covered many miles within the UK. In 1969 he organised for the 'Flying Scotsman' to be shipped to the United States for an extensive tour.

The following interview was made as part of the National Archive of Railway Oral History project (NAROH). This was a programme funded by the Friends of the NRM and the Heritage Lottery Fund to record the experiences of railway workers, and it ran from 2000 to 2003. Although Alan Pegler had never actually worked for the railway himself, he was chosen for interview because of the important role he had played in railway preservation, particularly of the 'Flying Scotsman' and the Festiniog Railway in North Wales.

Hugh Gould was a member of the volunteer interview team for NAROH and he worked for the railway, between 1956 and 1988, rising from working as a passenger guard during the summer months to manager of British Rail sectors. He was himself the subject of one of the NAROH interviews.

Q: What made you decide to go for 'Flying Scotsman' in the first place?

A: Well, various reasons. First of all, it was one of the first engines I'd seen at close quarters. I used to go down to Barnby Moor and Sutton from a very, very small age, I mean, sort of, you know, pushed in my pram or whatever it was, when, when I was very, very small indeed. And the first engine I saw really sort of close up was 4472, at the Wembley Exhibition, 1924 or 5, I don't know which year it was, but it would either have been 4 or 5 because I was born in 1920, so I was either 4 or 5 years old. And able to sort of have a look at this engine. I think I was actually able to climb into the cab, but that may be sort of thinking, wishful thinking over the years, I certainly imagined that I did, but I mean that had been the sort of for, for me the 'special engine'. Then of course in 1928, by that time I was an eight year old, and reasonably with-it as regards railways, and they started running the train of course, the first non-stop run, May 1st 1928, with a corridor-tender and all the press photographs were of 4472 with the corridor-tender. And one way and another, then of course, a few years after that, touching the 100 mile an hour. I often wonder how much they sort of had to bend the graph, but anyway they managed to stretch it to a 100 miles an hour for about 500 yards apparently —

Q: Anyway, when 'Scotsman' was saved, there was a second tender fitted, wasn't there?

A: No, not immediately, no. It was 1966, I got the second tender, and that was very largely thanks to having struck a very nice friendship with Terry Miller, and Terry Miller, of course, was again old L.N.E.R. or Eastern Region or whatever, and he turned out to have very great regret, as I did of the un-streamlined Gresley Pacific was going to be preserved because of course, the edict was you know, a particular design by a particular locomotive designer. So a Gresley Pacific, if you're going to have one at all it had to be 'Mallard', which I wouldn't argue with at all but that did mean, as you know that at one fell swoop all the unstreamlined ones were going to go. And again, I can't remember who was the General Manager then, I don't think it was Bird, but I did let it be known to the powers that be on the Eastern Region that if it got to the point where 'Flying Scotsman' was actually going to be scrapped, to please let me know because I might like to intervene and do something about it. And they'd started in Scotland by then these little ads in the papers SOS, Save our Scotsman, and all this sort of thing, but they were, I think, they weren't terribly well organised. They were, I think, probably the sort of forerunners of the present Gresley Society.

Q: Oh yes.

A: A couple of chaps in Scotland acting on behalf of the Gresley Society, but it got to the point in December 1962, I got a letter, I remember it very well, the first week of December, but the people in Scotland they needed £3,000, they had only raised about £1,000 and they hadn't got a hope of raising the rest in the time they'd got and if I wanted to do something about it, I'd have to move pretty quick. So I took the hint, and I did exactly that, I went straight up to Scotland, met the two chaps who'd been running this appeal, told them what I had in mind and I said, 'You're not going to make it, are you?' and they said rather sadly, 'No, I'm afraid we're not.' So I said, 'Well, look,' I said, 'if you're prepared to send back the subscriptions that you received, I will buy it outright myself and,' I said, 'what I've actually got in mind is not only preserving it but trying to preserve it as a runner.' Well that, of course, gobsmacked them completely and I didn't know whether I'd get away with it or not, but they liked the idea and they didn't object to refunding the subscriptions they'd had. So that's how it was done and then it was simply a question of, you know, producing the £3,000 and then I was simply asked, 'When do you want to sort of take delivery?" and I said, 'Well, if you would put it on the 1.15 out of King's Cross

On 14 January 1963, Kings Cross Station, London, the 'Flying Scotsman' watched by enthusiasts leaves Kings Cross on its final run north from London to Doncaster under British Railways ownership. Mr Pegler was on the footplate, having just bought the locomotive for £3,000.

on the 14th of January and take it off at Doncaster, it could then go straight into the Works and be put back as LNER,' and they, they did exactly that for me.

Q: Interesting.

A: Put it on the 1.15 to Leeds and it came off at Doncaster.

Q: Yes.

A: No, it was, it was very good.

Q: Yes. They could be very helpful indeed.

A: Oh they were marvellous and they were so quick about it too, I mean -

Q: Yes.

A: The time it takes to do anything these days.

Q: Yes.

A: Absolutely amazing.

Q: Yes.

A: And of course Terry Miller, I mean, he'd been such a help in the background, I mean God Almighty, I mean, I would hardly dare, I mean the – but I mean I wouldn't have dared then. I mean I got this, this whole thing done you know, the purchase, two trial runs to Peterborough and back with 11 coach trains, replacement of the double-chimney with a single-chimney, not because I objected to double-chimneys but simply because Terry Miller and I had decided between us, that if we were going to have an A3, it couldn't go back to 1923 and have it as an A1, but what you could do was have an, a typical unstreamlined Gresley Pacific, which really would be a sort of 1930s A3, and that's what we went for. And of course, only one Humorous ever had a double-chimney, or might have had two, but I think there was only about one out of 79 or 80, so it wouldn't have been typical to have a double-chimney, somebody was quoting it just the other day, on a film I was, a video that had just been put, had been put on sale and the present Chief Engineer of 'Flying Scotsman' is working for Tony Marchant, very nice chap but he's done the commentary on this latest video, saying, 'Alan Pegler didn't like this double-chimney, so he had it.' It's nothing to do with it, he'd missed the point completely. So, I'm, I'm going to have that sound track altered. No point in putting it on sale like this, completely stupid.

Q: That's clear.

A: Anyway, anyway. There we go. But that was the reason that that, that was done, getting, getting as more authentic as we could. And authenticity à la 1930s, as I say was certainly, was good old Humorous running around, but certainly the average Gresley unstreamlined didn't have a double-chimney, of course it didn't.

Q: No, no. Well, quite a number latterly, but only in the last few years.

A: Only in the last few years.

Q: Yes.

A: Yes.

Q: That's right. So in the '60s you were able to run her?

A: From the time I bought her, they had to have a date on the agreement, the heads of agreement had to come into force at a certain time, so I had these two trial runs while she was still theoretically I suppose, was still a BR engine but nevertheless the agreement was made, well anyway Terry worked it one way or another and finally we had to get the engine up to London because the first trip that I wanted, that I wanted the engine to do was for the Ffestiniog Railway Society, so that was going to be out of Paddington of all places, up to Ruabon of all places, in North Wales, where we were going to reverse, or the train was and go, well what is the line across to Bala, you know going through Llangollen that line, over to Barmouth your viaduct, that's the way we used to go on the Ffestiniog Special every year and so that was going to be on the, what was it. the 20th April, 20th April 1963, so the agreement was actually dated the 16th

April, simply because it was my birthday. I thought what a good day to have it, we said, "We've got to have a date on the agreement, what date shall we put on?" I said, "Well, make it the 16th April," which they did. So then it was my locomotive and so the first trip as officially a private locomotive was on the Ffestiniog service Paddington to Ruabon 20th April 1963.

Q: And many more to follow.

A: And many more to follow, not an awful lot in the first year, the next one was four weeks later, we ran from Lincoln to Southampton, which was an interesting one, that was all under the auspices of the Gainsborough, Gainsborough Model Railway Society.

Q: Oh yes.

A: I'm still President of that.

Q: Aha.

A: And I'm going off to their, their annual dinner next month. But … a very, very go-ahead organisation and they organise these trips brilliantly and they've got a lot of people from the – well Lincoln, Retford, Gainsborough, the area and the trains were very, very well patronised and we went down to Southampton in very good order indeed and … I remember so well we got coal in Southampton which was much, much smaller coal than we'd ever had before, well not that we'd ever had before, we'd only just started running, but it was much more than the, than the average fireman was used to seeing, and it was a coal called Ollerton Brights and Ollerton Brights were a fairly small coal, but anyway, it was a very – it worked a treat, no trouble at all, so we, we ran very well on that and got all the way back home in very good order, no trouble at all. But those were the first two trips.

Q: Yes.

A: Yeah.

Q: So she ran until … when ?

A: Well, ran on BR tracks until the autumn of 1969, but … by 1966 … it was getting to the point where there were jolly few sets of water troughs left –

Q: Yes.

A: Aand very few water columns left, and I had a long discussion with Terry Miller as to what to do and I suggested the idea of getting a second tender, and I said, I said, 'If I do get a second tender I want that to be a corridor tender as well so that I can get through,' and so he then started trying to find a second tender and he had a hell of a job finding one, and he found one eventually, not in very good nick up in Aberdeen.

Q: Oh yes.

A: That had been attached to number 34 which I think in – by then was 'Lord Farringdon' wasn't it?

Q: 'Farringdon' yes.

A: So he got hold of this tender, but it needed an awful lot of work doing on it, and the running gear wasn't in very good shape, so it was quite a big job getting the tender into shape to run at all and then converting the, you know, basically converting the coal space to water only. It ended up – I mean there wasn't all that big a capacity, but it was a capacity of about 6,000 gallons, so 6,000 gallons added to the 5,000 in the conventional tender and 11,000 gallons which was – made a hell of a difference, of course, and then I got this idea in '66, I'd really got it with the idea of being able to do the long drag without a stop, Leeds to Carlisle, and I thought, well, that'll just give it plenty of margin, not having to mess about with water stops, but that was becoming a fairly favourite route.

Q: Yes.

A: – of mine as you can imagine. Bashing over long –

Q: Yes, yes.

A: – of … the long – the long drag and all that. So that was what it was it done for and then, of course, having got it, the tender, and finding that it all worked all right I was then thinking about the original non-stop in 1928, and I thought, 'Well if I leave it till the 50th anniversary, in 1998, probably were – 19 whatever it was, eight – there probably won't be a hope in hell, that probably the troughs will have all gone by then, but if we made it the 40th anniversary in 1968, we could probably just about get away with it, with the three sets of water troughs that were still left.' So that was all put in the pipeline and Terry was entirely in favour of that and, as you know, we did it.

…

A: And apparently there are a lot of things that have come out in the wash since, but I mean, there were apparently there were all sorts of dirty work going in high places, whether people were having bets, I don't know, but you know, on the northbound journey we only got one decent pickup out of three, and when we were getting … near to the Scottish border, it was really – I was very, very worried that we wouldn't be able to go on, but we'd got a road tanker at Berwick just in case, and unfortunately we'd arranged all sorts of cunning signals if we did need to stop for the water tanker, and very unfortunately indeed, I think it was at Lucker, funnily enough, there's a station at Lucker, some idiot

Alan Pegler in the cab of 'Flying Scotsman' in 1987.

photographer was lying on his tummy on the platform to get a sort of really impressive picture of the train, so the driver seeing this fool lying on the platform was whistling like mad, and the signalman thought it was him crowing that we needed water at Berwick, so when we approached over the border bridge we were all set for the loop line, and of course the last thing we wanted to do was go into the loop and – so the wretched fireman, we got down to walking pace, the fireman was able to sprint ahead get on the teleprinter – 'Damn, we don't need the water keep us going,' so we just got the signal off into – had to go right round the – through the loop and out and out the other.

Q: Out the other end.

A: – passed the bloody 4000 gallons of water, dear oh dear oh dear, and of course when we finally got into Edinburgh, first thing I did, climb up on the, on the two tenders and really it was, it was – we'd just what we'd got in the boiler ... we really were – touch and go.

2

THE FLYING SCOTSMAN
PIANO SOLO

GEORGE SCOTT-WOOD

George Scott-Wood was born in 1903 and by the 1920s he had made a career in popular music. In 1934 he started a jazz group and by 1940 had started his own accordion band. George was a prolific composer and amongst the many works he wrote was The Flying Scotsman *which he wrote in 1950.*

LOCOMOTIVE PRACTICE and
PERFORMANCE of the 'FLYING SCOTSMAN'

O. S. NOCK, B.Sc., M.I.C.E., M.I.Mech.,E., M.I.Loco.E.

(Taken from The Railway Magazine *December 1965)*

Oswald Stevens Nock was an engineer and railway historian. He was born in 1905 and submitted his first article in 1929, to the Institute of Mechanical Engineers. He became a regular contributor to *The Railway Magazine* and his first book was published in 1945. From then on he produced almost two new titles every year. After his retirement in 1970, his output increased to five. He died on 21 September 1994.

When the steam age is finally ended in Great Britain and enthusiasts of future generations come to regard our own times in more distant retrospect, I wonder if they will sometimes debate among themselves as to which was the most famous steam locomotive of all time. The *Royal Scot*, the *King George V*, and *Mallard* would all be on the short list, and if one included earlier years such a list would undoubtedly include *Hardwicke*, Stirling's eight-footer No. 1, and Daniel Gooch's broad-gauge *Lord of the Isles*. But among them all – by the sheer magic of the name, and the association of engine with the title of one of the longest established and best known trains in the world – Sir Nigel Gresley's 'Flying Scotsman' will always hold a unique place in our affections.

Last month, in *The Railway Magazine*, reference was made to the part engine No. 4472 played in the working of the "Welsh Mystery Flyer". Other things being equal, 'Flying Scotsman' might have seemed a strange choice for such a duty. Equally, one could argue, "what's in a name?" I once travelled over nearly 200 miles of English railway in the "Irish Mail" behind a Scottish engine with a Welsh driver! This was from Euston to Chester, when the engine was *Gordon Highlander*, driven by the redoubted Harry Jones of Holyhead. But in her new-found youth 'Flying Scotsman' has travelled far beyond the confines of the former L.N.E.R. system, and nowadays one would not be the least surprised to see her turn up at Dover, Fishguard, or Barrow-in-Furness. Her recent excursions have thus prompted me to recall some of her past exploits, both recent and in the days of her real youth on the East Coast main line.

Engine No. 1472 as she originally was – 1472 N to be strictly correct, for she was not quite old enough to be born a Great Northern engine – was a picked unit from the outset. At first she was unnamed, and stationed at Doncaster for working the heavy Leeds expresses to and from Kings Cross. After the grouping, with Mr. H.N. Gresley, as he was then, appointed as Chief Mechanical Engineer of the L.N.E.R., it might have seemed a foregone conclusion that for future standards the Gresley Pacific design would have been preferred to the Raven. But in the summer of 1923 a comprehensive series of dynamometer-car trial runs was carried out between Doncaster and Kings Cross, to compare the two, and the engine chosen to represent the Great Northern design was No. 1472.

It might be argued that the latter was favoured by working over its own line, whereas the North Eastern men who worked the Raven Pacific No. 2400 had to learn the road. But the 10.51 up from Doncaster and the 17.45 down were incomparably the hardest turns on the entire L.N.E.R. system, and in a trial of strength they were obvious choices.

Engine No. 1472 was then in her original condition, with short-lap, short-travel valves, and so far as haulage capacity was concerned it was a very close fight between the two locomotives. But in coal consumption, even with short-lap valves, the advantage quite definitely lay with No. 1472. Quite apart from Gresley's natural preference for his own design, the test results justified the choice of the G.N. rather than the N.E. Pacific for the future standard. In passing, it is of interest to recall that the engineer in charge of the Darlington dynamometer car on those trials was R.A. Smeddle, who many years later became Chief Mechanical Engineer of the Western Region of British Railways. In actual running, however, the North Eastern Pacific did some very fine work, and the enthusiasts of the Gresley Society have recently published some logs, prepared from the actual dynamometer car records. By their courtesy I am able to reproduce two of these herewith.

In **Table I** are set out comparative runs by engines 1472 and 2400 on the 10.51 Doncaster to Kings Cross. Both engines had identical loads, but the North Eastern run was made on a Wednesday, when the train made an extra intermediate stop at Newark. It must be admitted that on the basis of these two runs the honours are overwhelmingly on the side of the North Eastern. The opening run to Retford set the pace for the entire trip, with such a notable difference in speeds at Pipers Wood summit as 45 and 51½ m.p.h., and No. 2400 was driven extremely hard from the Newark stop to make a really splendid time of 19 min. 25 sec. over the 14.6 uphill miles to Grantham. Again No. 1472 was "left standing" on the ascent to Stoke Box. Both engines were steaming freely, and once over the summit the Great

TABLE I

L.N.E.R.: 10.51 DONCASTER – KINGS CROSS

PACIFIC TRIALS: JUNE – JULY, 1923

Engine No.			1472		2400	
Design			G.N.R.		N.E.R.	
Load, tons (e/f)						
Doncaster – Grantham			453/485		453/485	
Grantham – Kings Cross				483/520		483/520
Dist.		Sch.	Actual	Speeds	Actual	Speeds
Miles		min.	m. s.	m.p.h.	m. s.	m.p.h.
0.0	DONCASTER		0 00	—	0 00	—
4.6	Rossington		7 36	50½	7 07	53
6.5	Milepost 149½		9 55	45	9 11	51½
12.0	Ranskill		15 41	63	14 24	68
			—	—	sigs.	—
17.4	RETFORD	21	21 27	—	20 26	—
4.6	Milepost 134		8 25	39½	8 05	41½
11.2	Crow Park		14 58	75	14 25	74
18.5	NEWARK	21	21 23	64	21 17	—
23.2	Claypole		26 04	58	7 29	53
27.1	Hougham		30 17	53	11 39	56
28.9	Barkston		32 32	42½*	13 43	50*
33.1	GRANTHAM	38	38 30	—	19 25	—
5.5	Stoke Box (Mp 100)		12 02	35	10 01	43½
8.4	Corby		15 23	65	13 05	65
13.3	Little Bytham		19 36	74	17 12	76½
16.9	Essendine		22 25	77	19 55	79
20.7	Tallington		25 31	74	22 56	74½
29.1	PETERBOROUGH	33	34 00	—	31 27	—
3.8	Yaxley		6 33	53	6 39	51½
7.0	Holme		9 47	63	9 55	62½
12.9	Abbots Ripton		15 45	50½	16 00	47½
17.5	HUNTINGDON	20	20 36	68	20 50	73
20.4	Offord		23 10	68	23 16	73
24.7	St. Neots		27 18	56	27 04	60
28.9	Tempsford		31 31	63	31 03	65½
32.3	Sandy		34 51	58	34 13	62½
35.3	Biggleswade		37 51	60	37 03	63
39.3	Arlesey		42 19	57	41 13	61
44.5	HITCHIN	48	48 07	47½	46 34	51
47.8	Stevenage		52 46	42	50 55	44½
51.4	Knebworth		57 06	49	55 04	51
			sigs.	36	—	—
58.7	HATFIELD	64	66 41	56	62 04	71
63.7	Potters Bar		72 43	49½	66 51	61
67.3	New Barnet		75 40	65	69 58	74½
			p.w.s.	44	p.w.s.	slight
71.4	Wood Green		81 16	60	73 35	73½
73.9	Finsbury Park		83 47	—	75 38	68½
76.4	KINGS CROSS	84	87 37	—	79 24	—

*Min. speed at Peascliffe Tunnel

Northern engine ran well enough; but Driver Blades and Fireman Fisher were really flailing No. 2400!

Out of Peterborough the driver of No. 1472 used a wider opening of the regulator than hitherto, and for once made the faster start. The minimum speed of 50½ m.p.h. at Abbots Ripton was excellent; but once past this point No. 2400 drew ahead, and with some splendid running had gained a lead of 2 min. on passing Knebworth. The report shows that this engine was at wing-off on passing Stevenage summit. Engine 1472 was worked in 40 per cent cut-off throughout, with the regulator opening varied to give the adjustments of power output required by the rise and fall of the road. Between Peterborough and Knebworth the steam-chest pressures were 140 lb. per sq. in. on Abbots Ripton bank; 110 at Tempsford; 135 on Stevenage bank; and 107 before Knebworth. The very fast approaches to Kings Cross will be noted, with both engines making times of less than 4 min. over the final 2½ miles in from Finsbury Park.

In this connection a good story is told of Driver Blades when he was learning the road before these trials. He was rather horrified at the speed his Great Northern colleagues ran down through the tunnels, and back on his native Tyneside after one spell of road-learning he exclaimed–in a translation of his Doric – "One of those blighters will land in Piccadilly Circus one day." But Blades was always an apt pupil, and the log in Table I shows that he learned to approach Kings Cross as fast as any of the G.N. men. Quite apart from the finish, this is by far the finest run I have ever seen with one of the Raven Pacifics.

Reverting to engine No. 1472, following her sojourns at the British Empire Exhibition at Wembley in 1924 and 1925 she went back to Doncaster shed, and although now dignified with the name 'Flying Scotsman' she did not work on the train itself. Then, following the interchange trial with the G.W.R. in 1925, the valve gear of the Gresley Pacifics was modified, and their performance – and coal consumption – was confirmed. 'Flying Scotsman' was modified in 1928, in time to work the inaugural Edinburgh non-stop. She, together with 4476, *Royal Lancer*, were equipped with corridor tenders, and went to Kings Cross shed. I never clocked 4472 on the "non-stop", but in 1933 I enjoyed a grand trip behind her on the up "Scotsman", which I joined at Darlington.

This run is set out in **Table II**. It was made just after the Whitsun holiday, and the train was crowded. I travelled in the same compartment as a Darlington driver and fireman who were going to pick up a Scarborough excursion working at York. The fireman was a cheery soul, and was soon in conversation with all of us passengers. It was a

TABLE II

L.N.E.R.: DARLINGTON – YORK
Load: 16 coaches; 528 tons tare, 565 tons full
Engine: 4472, 'Flying Scotsman'

Dist.		Sch.	Actual	Speeds
Miles		min.	m. s.	m.p.h.
0.0	DARLINGTON	0	0 00	—
2.6	Croft Spa		4 57	53½
5.2	Eryholme		7 56	51½
10.4	Danby Wiske		13 02	66½
14.1	NORTHALLERTON	17	16 29	64½
17.5	Otterington		19 29	72½
21.9	THIRSK	24	23 02	75
26.1	Sessay		26 32	71
28.0	Pilmoor		28 10	70½
30.7	Raskelf		30 27	73
32.9	Alne		32 13	75
34.4	Tollerton		33 25	74
38.6	Beningbrough		36 54	72
41.1	Milepost 3		39 01	71½
42.5	Poppleton Junc.		40 18	—
			sig. stop	
			41 28	—
44.1	YORK	46	47 00	—

*Net time: 43½ min.

hot day, and we had not gone far before he remarked, with some feeling, "I shouldn't like to fire this thing!" Naturally my stop-watching attracted attention, and as our speed with this huge train of sixteen coaches climbed into the "seventies", his eyes grew round with wonder: "Aye and he's going through to London too," was his further comment.

This was a run in the characteristic style of Driver Sparshatt and Fireman Webster, who had No. 4472 for so long. As the log shows, they worked this 565-ton train up to 75 m.p.h. on little easier than level track at Thirsk, and repeated this maximum, on an even slighter gradient near Alne. When the old North Eastern Railway booked the 13.09 from Darlington to York in 43 min., and

claimed the fastest start-to-stop run in Great Britain, one hardly imagined that one day that timing would be virtually kept with a 565-ton load. The rest of the long journey to Kings Cross involved a less strenuous effort, because the schedule was then 92 min. for the 82.6 miles to Grantham and 116 min. for the final 105.5 miles. On both sections engine and crew improved comfortably on booked time, though a double-home turn of this length could never be described as *easy*.

Another excellent run of pre-war vintage was that detailed in **Table III**, on the 17.45 down from Kings Cross. After the "Silver Jubilee" was put on, and the top-link crews took their turns in driving the new streamlined "A4s," the older engines were no longer confined to their regular crews on the Newcastle runs, and on this occasion No. 4472 was worked by Driver Ellis and Fireman Luty – another first-class pair. It was a dirty night in December, and the engine was slipping at intervals on the long rise to Potters Bar. Then came a succession of checks through Hatfield, and it was not until we were over Woolmer Green summit that normal speed began to be run. Then No. 4472 was taken along like the wind, covering the 40.8 miles from Stevenage to Holme in 33 min. 50 sec. – an average of 72½ m.p.h.

At the time the engine still had a boiler carrying a pressure of 180 lb. per

TABLE III

L.N.E.R.: 5.45 p.m. KINGS CROSS-GRANTHAM
Load: 15 coaches; 467 tons tare, 505 tons full
Engine: 4472, 'Flying Scotsman'

Dist.		Sch.	Actual		Speeds
Miles		min.	m.	s.	m.p.h.
0.0	KINGS CROSS	0	0	00	—
2.6	Finsbury Park		7	39	—
5.0	Wood Green		10	48	54½
12.7	Potters Bar		21	18	35
		sigs.	5		
17.7	HATFIELD	25	28	37	—
		sigs.	5		
23.5	Woolmer Green		38	43	35
28.6	Stevenage		44	52	57
31.9	HITCHIN	39	47	49	76½
35.7	Three Counties		50	39	83½
41.1	Biggleswade		54	43	80½
44.1	Sandy		57	00	75½
47.5	Tempsford		59	38	78
51.7	St. Neots		63	12	68
56.0	Offord		66	49	72/69
58.9	HUNTINGDON	62	69	18	72
63.5	Abbots Ripton		73	56	55½
	(min)				
69.4	Holme		78	42	79½
76.4	PETERBOROUGH	80	85	41	25
79.5	Werrington Junc.		90	48	55½
84.8	Tallington		96	07	65
88.6	Essendine		99	46	61/65
92.2	Little Bytham		103	15	60
97.1	Corby		108	38	
52½/55					
100.1	Stoke Box		112	08	49
		sigs.		—	
105.5	GRANTHAM	114	119	06	—

*Net time: 111 min

sq. in. (class "A1") and the high sustained speed on the easier stretches, such as Sandy to Tempsford, was as notable as the maxima down the 1 in 200 banks – 83½ m.p.h. at Three Counties, and 79½ m.p.h. at Holme. By this fine running 3 min. of the arrears at Hitchin had been recovered by the time the train passed through Peterborough, and some excellent work followed on the long adverse stretch to Stoke summit. On the gradual approach grades speed was sustained at between 60 and 65 m.p.h., and we were well on to the main ascent of 1 in 200 – at Little Bytham Station in fact – before speed fell below 60 m.p.h. Then nearly six miles of 1 in 200 did not bring us below 52½ m.p.h.; there was a rally to 55 m.p.h. past Corby; and the last three miles to the summit, inclined at 1 in 178, were cleared at 49 m.p.h. A signal check outside Grantham cost a further minute, but the net time was not more than 111 min.

The 'Flying Scotsman' and her regular crew Driver Sparshatt and Fireman Webster, were chosen for the experimental high-speed runs to and from Leeds on November 30, 1934. Thus, to her participation in the dynamometer-car trials against the North Eastern, to her sojourns at Wembley, and her inauguration of regular non-stop running between Kings Cross and Edinburgh, the famous engine was selected for the first trials towards the brilliant streamline age on the L.N.E.R. On that occasion a schedule of 165 min. had been laid down for the non-stop run of 185.8 miles from Kings Cross to Leeds Central. A load of no more than four coaches was taken on the outward journey, making no more than 147 tons gross behind the tender. This train was treated with positive derision. On the fastest stretch a maximum speed of 95 m.p.h. was attained; Stoke summit was cleared at a minimum of 81¼ m.p.h.; and eventually Leeds was reached 13 min. early – in 151 min. 56 sec. from Kings Cross.

Encouraged by this very fast running the load was increased to six coaches for the return trip, 207½ tons gross behind the tender. Another magnificent run was made, including, for the first time on authentic record, a maximum speed of 100 m.p.h. descending from Stoke towards Peterborough. Naturally the overall time was not so fast as on the down journey; but a total of 157 min. 17 sec. from Leeds to Kings Cross with a load of 207 tons was an outstanding achievement. On this one day 'Flying Scotsman' had covered an aggregate total distance of 250 miles at an average speed of 80 m.p.h., and while her driver deserved every commendation for his handling of the engine, Fireman Webster, on the round trip, had shovelled no less than nine tons of coal in the running time of a shade over five hours.

Thirty years later it is good to have this famous engine still with us and, thanks to the enterprise of Mr. Alan Pegler, in superb working order. It is true that she is now an "A3", but that form of rebuilding was applied to all the original Gresley 180-lb. Pacifics. In her present form she has travelled over some distinctly unusual routes. A very interesting round trip was recently made from London to Weymouth and back – outward via the Southern route, and returning over the Great Western. No very exceptional running was made over any section, having regard to the moderate load, by previous East Coast standards, of only 255 tons. Nevertheless, from a stop at Woking the 49.2 miles to passing Eastleigh took only 52½ min., and the 28.3 miles from Southampton to Bournemouth Central were covered in 30 min. 31 sec. start to stop.

On the return trip some excellent running was made between Westbury and Reading – indeed Savernake summit, 25.5 miles from the start, was passed in 25 min. 3 sec. Up the 1 in 222 gradient from Lavington speed did not fall below 60 m.p.h., and after a maximum of 75 m.p.h. near Pewsey, the lowest speed at Savernake was 68 m.p.h. This, although very good with a driver and fireman working a locomotive that was strange to them, was by no means a record for trains of this weight, and I have clocked a "Castle" to beat these times and speeds substantially with an Ocean Mail special from Plymouth. I mention the matter of record-breaking because the final run I am about to describe was most of its distance of a still higher order. Before leaving the Weymouth round trip I must express my thanks to Mr. T. M. Bagwith, for sending me copies of the logs he compiled.

So I come in conclusion to the "Welsh Mystery Flyer", the trip organised by

The Railway Magazine, and described in the November issue. As briefly mentioned in that issue 'Flying Scotsman's' part in the proceedings came to a premature end, in circumstances quite inexplicable, if one regarded them as a normal engine "failure". Nevertheless it is with what was actually achieved rather than the mystery of that failure that I am now concerned.

In the last years of steam on the crack trains the "Bristolian" was booked to pass Didcot in 46 min. and Swindon in 67 min. The "Welsh Mystery Flyer" was allowed 67 min. to the stop for water at Swindon, with a load almost exactly the same as that of the steam-hauled "Bristolian". But the L.N.E.R. engine could have been handicapped by the stipulated maximum speed limit of 80 m.p.h. at all points. As on all her recent journeys the engine was in charge of local men, on the "Welsh Mystery Flyer" with a Southall crew, whose experience of really fast running must have been very limited. Some prospective passengers were speculating as to how the young fireman would cope with the wide firebox; but, of course, Southall men are now quite familiar with the "BR9" 2-10-0s, albeit on freight trains.

It was an ideal morning for fast running – clear, and practically no wind. The start was no more than moderate, no doubt while the men were getting the "feel" of the engine. But by Southall speed was up to 66½ m.p.h., and from there onwards we continued at a truly cracking pace. To indicate something of our prowess, comparison may be made of the time over the 22¾ miles from West Drayton to Reading, with that achieved on a celebrated Western Region occasion, namely the "dress rehearsal" for the restored high-speed "Bristolian", on April 30, 1954. The load included the dynamometer car; Mr. K.W.C. Grand rode on the footplate, and every effort was made to secure a fast run. With a "King" class engine and a load of 260 tons the time from West Drayton to Reading was 17 min. 40 sec. – an average speed of 77.3 m.p.h. On the "Welsh Mystery Flyer" the gallant 4472 took only 16 min. 45 sec. – 81.6 m.p.h.!

The pace from West Drayton onwards was indeed remarkably steady – just like a "Castle" in its very prime, except that a "Castle" would have had difficulty in running so fast with a load of 255 tons. The usual speed of the "Bristolian" on a top-class run was 77 or 78 m.p.h. on this part of the line. On the Great Western record down run of June 6, 1932, with engine No. 5005, *Manorbier Castle*, and a load of 210 tons, the time from West Drayton to Reading was 16 min. 36.4 sec., an average of 82.5 m.p.h. That 'Flying Scotsman' should have come so near to this was truly a remarkable feat, and in continuing to Cholsey the correspondence was even

LONDON & NORTH EASTERN RAILWAY
LONDON
KINGS CROSS
THE FLYING SCOTSMAN

LONDON & NORTH EASTERN RAILWAY
EDINBURGH
WAVERLEY
THE FLYING SCOTSMAN

FLYING SCOTSMAN-
AUS. STEAM 1988
COVER CARRIED

Centenary of
THE FLYING SCOTSMAN
1862-1962

The Flying Scotsman neither gives the oldest train service in the world, nor is it the oldest named train. But a hundred years ago, a train left London, King's Cross, for Edinburgh, at ten o'clock in the morning. This became the down train's normal time. At the same moment another train left Edinburgh, Waverley, for London and until 1876 this up train's time was variable. But otherwise, in the middle of the Plain of York, the trains passed one another at whatever were the full speeds of the period. They have been, and still remains, collectively The Flying Scotsman.

This great service began as a special Scotch Express and graduated through such titles as Flying Scotch Express and Flying Scotsman to The Flying Scotsman. During its century it has been worked by the most advanced and successful locomotives of the time. There has been something dynamic about engines of The Flying Scotsman. Although oil and electricity, not coal and water, now give motion, there is a connection with the very beginnings of railway motive power. The firm founded by George and Robert Stephenson in 1823 is today a part of the great English Electric organization, whence comes the powerful diesel-electric locomotive at the head of The Flying Scotsman we now know.

With one stop in the course of 393 miles, this train does the journey in six hours. It is a train with a great—and democratic—tradition. It is not for us a luxury priced but an ordinary train, carrying first and second-class passengers, serving all who come.

Wine List

The
FLYING SCOTSMAN
1862-1962

The Flying Scotsman

London   Edinburgh
Edinburgh   London

*This world-famous train has left
King's Cross at 10.0 a.m. since 1862*

closer: 12.5 miles in 9 min. 2 sec. and 9 min. 8 sec. respectively – averages of 83.0 and 82.2 m.p.h.

By this time all seemed set for a really astonishing start-to-stop time from Paddington to Swindon. I was reckoning that we stood an excellent chance of covering the 27½ miles from Cholsey to Milepost 76 in 21 min., which would have given 62½ min. from the start, and a possible 64½ min. to the stop. But it was on passing Cholsey that we felt that ominous jerk that marked the point of failure of the steam-chest cover. It was highly commendable in the circumstances that the crew managed to get from Didcot to Swindon in 27 min. and arrived only 5 min. late; in fact it was not until Steventon had been passed that the engine was really limping, and the 56½ miles from Paddington had taken only, 47¾ min. – 71 m.p.h. average. 'Flying Scotsman' had once again shown magnificent form, and, as I hope to describe later, she since again has had the chance to challenge the 1932 Great Western record.

TABLE IV

WESTERN REGION: PADDINGTON-SWINDON
The "Welsh Mystery Flyer"
Load: 7 coaches; 235 tons tare, 255 tons full
Engine: 4472, 'Flying Scotsman'

Dist.		Sch.	Actual		Speeds
Miles		min.	m.	s.	m.p.h.
0.0	PADDINGTON	0	0	00	—
1.3	Westbourne Park	4	3	27	—
5.7	Ealing Broadway		8	54	58
9.1	Southall	11	12	03	66½
11.0	Milepost 11		13	43	73
13.25	West Drayton		15	32	71
14.75	Iver		16	40	80
16.25	Langley		17	47	81
18.5	SLOUGH	18½	19	27	82
21.0	Burnham		21	18	80½
24.2	Maidenhead	23	23	39	82
27.0	Milepost 27		25	42	81½
29.0	Milepost 29		27	09	83
31.0	Twyford	28½	28	38	77
34.0	Milepost 34		30	54	80½
36.0	READING	32½	32	21	83
38.7	Tilehurst		34	17	81
41.5	Pangbourne		36	21	82½
44.75	Goring		38	43	82
48.5	Cholsey		41	29	80½
53.1	DIDCOT	45½	44	57	75
56.5	Steventon		47	47	70½
	Slowing			40	
66.5	Uffington	56	59	54	66
71.5	Shrivenham		64	41	—
76.0	Milepost 76		69	57	—
77.3	SWINDON	67	72	00	—

LOCOMOTIVE PRACTICE and PERFORMANCE
NON-STOP AGAIN!

O. S. NOCK, B.Sc., C.Eng., M.I.C.E., M.I.Mech.,E., M.I.Loco.E.
(Taken from The Railway Magazine *July 1968)*

In the May, 1968, issue of *The Railway Magazine* I recalled the running of the summer non-stop expresses that ran between Kings Cross and Edinburgh each season from 1928 to 1961, save for the intervention of the war years, 1940–47. The inauguration of so celebrated a service is always worthy of commemoration, and with one of the two engines actually involved still available, and in first class running trim, the temptation to try and do something special for the fortieth anniversary must have been well-nigh irresistible.

But with steam traction to end completely on British Railways in the autumn of this year, it is not merely a case of having a locomotive of suitable calibre available. Servicing facilities have been dismantled, access points for loading of coal dispensed with, and the chances of having suitable young enginemen who could fire a Pacific on such a lengthy duty not exactly rosy. It is not merely a question of stamina or firing skill; the keeping of a locomotive going, non-stop, over a run of nearly 400 miles, even with relays of

Crowds look on, and newsreel cameramen record the scene under the watchful eye of a policeman, as 'Flying Scotsman' prepares to leave Platform 10 at Kings Crosss, to repeat her non-stop run of 40 years earlier.

firemen, needs the experience gained in years of hard training and regular footplate working.

Nevertheless, through the enthusiasm and enterprise of Alan Pegler, the owner of the Gresley Pacific engine No. 4472, 'Flying Scotsman', and the whole-hearted co-operation of British Railways, and the Locomotive Club of Great Britain, No. 4472 once again left No. 10 Platform at Kings Cross at 10.00 on May 1, 1968, once again bound for Edinburgh – and it was hoped, and planned for, non-stop. The preliminary discussions, and the detailed organisation that preceded this historic departure, would fill a whole volume of *The Railway Magazine*, let alone one article of mine. It is enough to say here that the best thanks of all railway enthusiasts are due to all those who took part in this planning, and who eventually had the great satisfaction of seeing No. 4472 enter Waverley Station in 7¾ hr. from Kings Cross, without the wheels having stopped turning. I say this rather than "non-stop", because there were three moments on the journey when the speed was so reduced that a stop seemed absolutely inevitable.

The overriding problem was that of water supply. Three sets of troughs on the Great Northern line have been removed, those at Langley, Werrington and Newark. Three at present remain, namely Scrooby, Wiske Moor and Lucker. With a second tender and an initial supply of an extra 6,000 gallons, as compared with the conditions of 40 years ago, it might be thought that no further difficulties would be experienced once Scrooby was reached; because then things would be no different from those regularly met by the "non-stop" in its long career with "A1", "A3" and "A4" engines.

Today, however, with the troughs used to no more than a limited extent, the chances of getting a really good "fill-up" at each were very much less than one hundred per cent, and as things turned out the dice seemed definitely loaded against us on May 1. The train load was kept down to seven coaches, with a tare weight of 250 tons, while in comparing conditions with those of 40 years ago, the extra tender added 59 tons, making a tare load of 309 tons behind the first tender. Both tenders are of the corridor type.

As on the first "non-stop", in May, 1928, the engine crews were from Kings Cross and Gateshead sheds, although today of course "Kings Cross" is no more than a nominal title now that "Top Shed" is dismantled. The crews in 1968 were Driver J. Hill, and Fireman R. Speller and A. Ramage, from Kings Cross, and Passed Fireman H. Heron, driving, and Passed Fireman S. Whittaker, firing, from Gateshead. On the footplate in turn were Chief Locomotive Inspector L. Richards, Eastern Region, and Headquar-

'Flying Scotsman' passes Newcastle Central and crosses Castle Junction with the 40th anniversary non-stop special train on May 1.

ters Locomotive Inspector G. Harland and on these two in particular rested the responsibility for making important decisions at different stages in the journey, as will be told later.

It was a privilege to travel on the train that day, and to have as fellow passengers Sir Nigel Gresley's elder daughter, Mrs. Godfrey, and her own son and daughter. Other old friends were Inspector A. Dixon, now retired, with whom I have covered many hundreds of miles on the footplate, and Driver E. Hailstone, one of the most celebrated East Coast drivers of the post-war era, whose regular engine at "Top Shed" was the pioneer Gresley streamlined Pacific *Silver Link*.

RIGHT: *The 'Flying Scotsman' leaving King's Cross station on 1 May 1968 to commemorate the 40th anniversary of the first non-stop run from London to Edinburgh in 1928.*

Even before we had turned a wheel out of Kings Cross it was evident that the occasion was to be made an outstanding one. The B.B.C. Television people had chartered one of the seven coaches of the train and their cheerful young director, cameraman, and continuity girls were preparing for a most comprehensive documentary film, in colour. Crowds massed at every conceivable vantage point, at the platform ends, alongside the engine yard, and over the portals of Gasworks Tunnels. We left simultaneously with the present *Flying Scotsman*, recalling the regular procedure with the two 4 p.m. departures of pre-war days, with the "Coronation" and the 4 p.m. Yorkshire express paralleling each other for the first hundred yards.

We took the slow line, duly slowing to cross over to the fast line at Finsbury Park, and in that exit from London we saw demonstrations of the extraordinary interest this run was arousing, in the almost continuous crowds of sightseers and well-wishers along the lineside. It would have been interesting to know the *acreage* of film exposed on us during the day, quite apart from all that the B.B.C. Television folks did.

I have dwelt rather on the accompaniments at the start, because they were all so deeply impressive; but by the time we passed Wood Green it was time to get down to the serious business of locomotive performance. The preliminaries were, however, enough to show the deep affection in which the steam locomotive is held, by an extraordinary number of people. Time had been allowed for the slow, photographic start out of Kings Cross, but we passed Wood Green at 55 m.p.h. and went in fine style up the long 1 in 200 to Potters Bar, topping the summit at 57 m.p.h. Then came a relaying slack at Hatfield, and thereafter the going was leisurely for a time to keep as close as possible to our timetable path. Any exuberance had to be restrained, because running ahead of time could easily have led to a signal stop, and with that all the prestige value of a non-stop run would have been lost.

The point-to-point time of 12 min. for the 14.8 miles from Sandy to Huntingdon was very sharp, however, and things were neatly judged by passing Sandy a minute early, and taking 13 min. on this stage. By this, inordinately hard work over a short section was avoided. The engine was clearly in splendid form from the way we stormed up Stukeley Bank, falling only from 68 to 63 m.p.h. in this 3.1 miles of 1 in 200, and we touched 76 m.p.h. at Connington South, before easing off for the stretch across the Fens.

Signals were all clear for us through Peterborough, and after passing Werrington on time we made a fine climb to Stoke, averaging 64.2 m.p.h. from Tallington to the summit box, with a minimum of 56½ m.p.h. This climbing makes an interesting comparison with an ordinary run of my own with engine 4472 on the 5.45 p.m. Newcastle express in 1936 when with a gross load of 505 tons we averaged 57.3 m.p.h.

We passed Grantham a little before time, but again this was intentional to offset another sharp allowance of 12 min. for the 14.6 miles on to Newark. Admittedly this latter is mostly downhill; but it would have demanded an average of 73 m.p.h. following recovery from the easy run through Grantham. Running as we did, a more even demand was kept on the boiler – a most important factor in securing economic performance, and minimum coal and water consumption. I need hardly add that the attainment of a maximum speed of 76 m.p.h. near Claypole was achieved on the easiest of steaming.

After a quiet run across the Trent valley there came another excellent climb, with a minimum speed of 56½ m.p.h. at Markham summit (Milepost 134). At this point we had covered 129 miles, from Wood Green, in 124 min. 53 sec., at an average speed of 62 m.p.h. This was excellent in itself, having regard to the intermediate slacks at Hatfield and Peterborough, but also because no advantage whatever had been taken of the traditional racing stretch of the old G.N.R. from Stevenage to Sandy.

So economically had the engine been working that by the time we passed Retford and were nearing the critical "pick-up" at Scrooby troughs the crew had not yet begun to draw on the water supply in the second tender. A distance of 140 miles had been covered on less than 6,000 gal. – only 42 gal. to the mile. While this splendid thermodynamic performance had been in progress, the train itself had been the object of extraordinary attention all along the line.

The B.B.C. Television helicopters were in constant attendance, often flying little higher than the tops of the trees; inside the train the cameramen, and others of the team, worked like Trojans, and in their frequent trips through the two corridor tenders, and their long vigils at open windows, got almost as begrimed as Alan Pegler and George Harland; while at every township and village organised parties of schoolchildren were waving ecstatically, old men doffed their caps, and toddlers were held high by their mothers to see the *steam* 'Flying Scotsman' pass.

To some of us in the train the very smoothness of our progress seemed almost too good to last. It was indeed! Although we recovered well from the Retford permanent-way check, there was consternation after Scrooby, where we scooped considerably less than 1,000 gallons. Speed had been carefully reduced to about 45 m.p.h., which is generally considered the optimum speed for a maximum pick-up;

and although with the supply in the second tender to draw upon we had plenty to get to Wiske Moor, if the poor pick-up at Scrooby was then repeated we should be in dire trouble. Before leaving that smooth and exhilarating start to the long run I should add that Fireman Speller had done the firing as far as Grantham, and there he was relieved by Fireman Ramage who continued to Aycliffe. Despite the Retford check we approached Doncaster well on time, and with clear signals throughout passed through some ¾ min. to the good.

Then misfortune struck, good and hard. Bentley Colliery "distant" was on. Speed was reduced to a crawl, and with continuous whistling we approached the box, where a crowd of platelayers were seen on the line. Obstinately the home signal remained on, and with speed down to less than walking pace Inspector Harland jumped down from the engine and *ran ahead* to learn there was a broken rail. By this timely and unprecedented action he obtained authority to proceed before we had actually stopped, and having passed at dead-slow speed over the fracture we all breathed again as speed was regained, and we bowled along the level towards Selby.

This check had cost us some five minutes in running, but there was no point in hurrying to regain the loss. There was an ample recovery mar-

gin between Selby and York, and to approach the latter the least fraction ahead of time would be asking for a stop. There was a very tight margin behind a Birmingham-Newcastle express. Actually things worked out to perfection; all signals were green for us, and once again the cynosure of all eyes – what a crowd too! – we passed through the great station within a few seconds of precise schedule time.

From the viewpoint of locomotive power output the continuation of the journey had few features of interest. The schedule allowed 94 min. for the ensuing 80.1 miles from York to Newcastle, and if there were some slight variations from that point-to-point allowance they were made in the interest of evening out the demands on the boiler. As before, a major point of interest became the amount of water likely to be scooped at Wiske Moor. Here we did much better than at Scrooby, collecting nearly 3,000 gal., and with beautifully judged firing and driving, and clear signals, we passed King Edward Bridge Junction and wound our way through Newcastle Central a minute early. That minute nevertheless very nearly cost us the non-stop run, for we got signals "on" at Manors, and only the most judicious crawling afterwards avoided a dead stand. Speed was down to 2 m.p.h. before the line was cleared for us.

By this time the weather had sadly

TABLE I
EAST COAST ROUTE
THE 40TH ANNIVERSARY NON-STOP: MAY 1, 1968
Load: 7 coaches, 250 tons tare behind second tender, 330 tons gross behind first tender
Engine: 4-6-2 No. 4472, 'Flying Scotsman',
Drivers: Hill (Kings Cross) Heron (Gateshead)

Dist.		Sch.	Actual		Speeds
Miles		min.	m.	s.	m.p.h.
0.0	KINGS CROSS	0	0	00	—
2.6	Finsbury Park	7½	9	37	—
5.0	Wood Green		13	37	55
12.7	Potters Bar	22	21	57	57
—			p.w.s.		68/15*
17.7	HATFIELD	27	27	30	—
25.0	Knebworth		35	32	70(max.)
31.9	HITCHIN	44	42	00	easy
44.1	Sandy	55	53	43	63½
47.5	Tempsford		56	43	75
51.7	St. Neots		60	28	68/72
58.9	Huntingdon	67	66	42	68
62.0	Milepost 62		69	32	63
69.7	Holme		75	45	76(max.)
76.4	PETERBOROUGH	83	83	10	—
79.5	Werrington Junc.	88	87	44	60
88.6	Essendine	97	95	55	69(max.)
97.1	Corby Glen		103	55	57/63
100.1	Stoke Box	108	106	53	56½
105.5	GRANTHAM	113	112	10	easy
109.7	Barkston S. Junc.	117	116	02	72
115.4	Claypole	120	45	76½	
120.1	NEWARK	125	124	43	eased
134.0	Milepost 134		138	30	56½(min.)
—			p.w.s.		
—	Scrooby	—			69½/48
156.0	DONCASTER	164	163	05	—
—	Bentley Colliery		sigs.		broken
				rail	
160.2	Shafteholme Junc.	169	171	50	—
174.4	SELBY	183	187	03	—
186.2	Chaloners Whin Junc.		201	06	—
188.2	YORK	205	204	45	—
197.9	Tollerton	217	217	04	57
210.4	Thirsk	228½	230	00	—
218.2	NORTHALLERTON	236	237	48	60/45
—			p.w.s.		15
227.1	Eryholme Junc.	248	248	50	—
232.3	DARLINGTON	256	257	40	—
245.2	Ferryhill	269½	271	05	68(max.)
254.3	DURHAM	279	280	51	—
264.5	Lamesley		291	32	73(max.)
267.7	King Edward Bridge Junc.	296	294	55	—
268.3	NEWCASTLE	299	297	55	—

* 'Speed restrictions

Dist.		Sch.	Actual		Speeds	
Miles		min.	m.	s.	m.p.h.	
			sigs.			
273.3	Forest Hall		308	45	—	
284.9	Morpeth	323	323	25	slow	
293.9	Chevington		335	37	easy	
303.1	Alnmouth	344	345	10	56	
307.7	Little Mill		350	32	49	
319.9	Belford	364	365	03	—	
333.9	Tweedmouth Junc.	387	386	55	—	
—			sigs.	—		
			prolonged			
335.2	BERWICK-UPON-TWEED		394	50	—	
340.8	Burnmouth		406	45	40	
—			p.w.s.		20	
351.5	Grantshouse 410	423	45	40		
358.9	Innerwick		431	03	75	
363.5	DUNBAR	424	435	08	60*	
369.2	East Linton		440	48	64	
374.9	Drem		445	37	73	
378.5	Longniddry		449	39	66/69	
386.6	Monktonhall Junc.		445	456	17	—
389.7	Portobello		449	459	15	—
392.7	EDINBURGH WAVERLEY		460	464	57	—

* Speed restrictions

deteriorated, and we ran through Northumberland in pouring rain. Speed was kept at the moderate level demanded by the schedule, and despite the episode at Manors we were only a minute down at Alnmouth.

We were now approaching the critical point of this later part of the journey, Lucker troughs. The possibility of our running short of water had loomed large in all the preparations for the trip, and a road tanker, with 4,000 gal., was standing in readiness in the goods yard at Berwick. If we did not get enough at Lucker there was this emergency supply, though it would of course have meant stopping. Lucker was passed, and shortly afterwards Pegler came back from the footplate with a look on his face that told its own tale. We had scooped up less than 1,000 gal. and, as he put it, he had left the experts on the footplate to judge whether they had enough to get through. It had been decided that if we needed water at Berwick a warning whistle would be given as we passed Beal, and hearing no such whistle we assumed Les Richards had decided he had enough to get through.

Approaching Tweedmouth the brakes went on, and, although we passed there dead on time, we commenced an agonisingly slow crawl over the Royal Border Bridge. The colour-light signals were on, and with

TABLE II
EAST COAST ROUTE
THE UP NON-STOP: SATURDAY, MAY 4, 1968
Load: 7 coaches, 250 tons tars behind second tender
330 tons gross behind first tender
Engine: 4-6-2 No. 4472, 'Flying Scotsman'
Drivers: Borlace (Gateshead)
Lunnis (Kings Cross)

Dist.		Sch.	Actual		Speeds
Miles		min.	m.	s.	m.p.h.
0.0	EDINBURGH WAVERLEY	0	0	00	
3.0	Portobello	6	6	14	—
6.1	Monktonhall Junc.	10	11	02	—
17.8	Drem	21	23	51	62
29.2	DUNBAR	31	34	08	73/58*
33.8	Innerwick		39	17	64
41.2	Grantshouse	48	48	17	43
57.5	BERWICK-UPON-TWEED		65	19	easy
58.8	Tweedmouth Junc.	68	67	07	—
—	Goswick		72	32	71
72.8	Belford	88	84	33	eased
89.6	Alnmouth	108	106	28	—
107.8	Morpeth	126	129	38	40*
114.5	Cramlington		137	40	58/52
124.4	NEWCASTLE	150	151	35	—
125.0	King Edward Bridge Junc.	153	153	12	—
128.2	Lamesley		157	03	60
138.4	DURHAM	170	169	20	—
147.5	Ferryhill	182	180	44	62(max.)
160.4	DARLINGTON	198	199	58	easing
—			p.w.s.	30	
165.6	Eryholme Junc.		207	59	—
170.8	Danby Wiske		213	01	70/48
174.5	NORTHALLERTON	213	216	57	61
182.3	Thirsk	220	223	19	80
193.3	Alne		231	58	74/80
—			sigs.		2
194.8T	ollerton	230	239	16	—
202.9	Skelton Box		247	14	72(max)
204.5	YORK	240	250	26	25*
214.2	Riccall		261	04	76
218.3	SELBY	256	265	44	40*
222.9	Templehirst		267	54	62
229.7	Moss		275	53	80
232.5	Shaftholme Junc.	273	278	16	58/73
236.7	DONCASTER	280	282	42	61
245.0	Bawtry		291	00	65(max.)
254.1	RETFORD	303	302	10	—
—			p.w.s.		30
272.6	NEWARK	322	324	30	easy
277.3	Claypole		329	14	60
283.0	Barkstone S. Junc.	334	334	55	57

Dist.		Sch.	Actual		Speeds
Miles		min.	m.	s.	m.p.h.
287.2	GRANTHAM	339	339	14	63
292.6	Stoke Box	346	344	53	50
304.1	Essendine	357	356	33	78(max.)
316.3	PETERBOROUGH	372	370	24	15*
333.8	Huntingdon	393	390	22	easy
341.0	St. Neots		398	04	56
348.6	Sandy	405	405	37	71
360.8	HITCHIN	416	416	27	62
364.1	Stevenage		420	05	54
375.0	HATFIELD	432	431	19	70(max.)
—			p.w.s.		20
380.0	Potters Bar	439	438	29	56
383.5	New Barnet		441	51	68
387.7	Wood Green		445	17	—
390.1	Finsbury Park	452	448	48	—
392.7	KINGS CROSS	458	455	32	—

*Speed restrictions

the whole area northwards to Burn-mouth remotely controlled from the Tweedmouth panel no amount of whistling or gesticulations from the footplate could hurry their clearance. We could only crawl on, but when Berwick was approached it was seen that the points were set for us to go through the goods line, beside that road tanker, in which, to quote Pegler, there were "four thousand gallons of lovely water."

As we turned off the main line heads were out from end to end of the train, despite the pouring rain, and then, to everyone's amazement and delight, old 4472 rode slowly, but determinedly right past that tanker, and continued on her way. There was one last breathless moment in this episode: the signals to let us out on to the main line remained steadfastly on. But the track-circuit lights on Tweedmouth panel must have

shown – just in time – that we were still on the move, and the outlet signal suddenly changed to green.

For the third time a dead stop had, by a hair's breadth, been avoided, and on this last occasion the loss of time had been more serious. We got under way again once more, up the 1 in 190 over the Border and into Scotland; but the 6.8 miles from Tweedmouth Junction to Burnmouth had taken no less than 19 min. 50 sec., and with a further permanent-way slack near Reston we topped the summit near Grantshouse nearly 14 min. late. There remained 41.2 miles to go and 38 min. left for a punctual arrival. Assured of ample water supply it could have been done, in spite of the overall speed limit of 75 m.p.h. throughout Scottish Region. But Inspector Richards, above all people, knew that he was cutting things fine, for water, and the engine was not pressed.

On this last stage there was another hazard. Even in the open country of the East Lothians there was one tight timetable margin. A diesel multiple-unit train from North Berwick was due to take the main line at Drem four minutes after our scheduled passing time. We passed Dunbar 11¼ min. late, and those "in the know" once again held their breaths until Drem "distant" was sighted. It was clear. More than this, we dashed through Drem at 70 m.p.h. to see, through steamed-up rain-slashed windows, that the d.m.u. had been held for us, and we had a clear road right into Waverley. With the help of a generous amount of recovery time from Portobello we were only 5 min. late in – in any case half an hour faster than the schedule time of 40 years ago. I must not dilate on the scenes that greeted our arrival. Waverley rang to the shrill welcoming notes of a pipe band; the Lord Provost was on the platform to meet us, with the Lady Provost; and later that evening Edinburgh Castle was floodlit in honour of the occasion.

This, however, is an article about locomotive performance, and a careful check-up on arrival showed that our total water consumption was a little under 14,000 gal. – only 35 gal. per mile. Of the checks experienced *en route* I estimate that Bentley cost us

5 min., Eryholme 3½ min., and Manors 3 min. Of course Berwick was by far the most severe, and cost about 14 min. The remaining three permanent-way slacks cost about 3½ min. between them, making up a total of 28 min. The net time can thus be set down as 437 min., a splendid average of 54 m.p.h.– NON-STOP. The engine was stabled for the night at Dunfermline, and on arrival there everything was found to be in perfect order, all bearings cool, and when being prepared for the next day's work, in all only two pints of oil were needed to replenish all three big ends and all three small ends, together with the motion pins.

It is interesting to compare the actual times made on the inaugural journey in 1928 with our own times, thus:

I was not able to participate in any more of the special running that week, and returned to Kings Cross by the "Night Scotsman" on May 1. Imagine my astonishment, after the previous day's proceedings, to read next morning in *The Times*, of all newspapers,

'FLYING SCOTSMAN'–NON-STOP

Date		1928 Time (min.)	1968 Time
Kings Cross	dep.	0	0
Peterborough	pass	84	83
Grantham	"	118	112
Doncaster	"	174	163
York	"	217	205
Newcastle	"	322	298
Berwick	"	410	395
Edinburgh	arr.	483	465

THIRSTY "SCOT" STOPS TO DRINK, heading a curiously ill-informed article in which readers were told that the 'Flying Scotsman' had to make three halts to take on water. From whom the Scottish correspondent of this usually most reliable newspaper gathered this nonsense is hard to imagine! Equally garbled was his reference to the record run on the last night of the 1895 race, which suggested that only one engine was then concerned.

It was learned afterwards that the water level in the troughs was at the lower level normally maintained for the diesels, and on Saturday, May 4, when the return trip was attempted non-stop, the water level was raised to full height, and with an ample water supply a very comfortable trip ensued. Through the kindness of Mr. C.F. Firminger of the L.C.G.B. I have been furnished with a very detailed log, a summary of which is set out in Table II herewith. There was one anxious moment, when adverse signals cut short a grand piece of high-speed running south of Northallerton, but other than that it was a triumphantly smooth and punctual trip.

Once again one notes the excellent hill-climbing, as in the minimum speed of 43 m.p.h. up the Cockburnspath bank, after four miles of 1 in 96, and the good going from Newark up to Stoke Box. For the most part, however, skilful enginemanship was being displayed to keep as close as possible to the scheduled timetable path. I am delighted to be able to set on record this splendid complementary run to the anniversary trip of May 1; the two together represent a triumph of organisation and enterprise, and yet another tribute to the work of Sir Nigel Gresley. It was delightful that his elder daughter and his grandchildren were able to participate, and to see for themselves and tremendously to enjoy the manifestations of interest and enthusiasm displayed throughout the entire trip, on both days of non-stop running.

On arrival at King's Cross on May 4, they had 4,000 gal. of water and more than two tons of coal in hand, thus showing that so long as the three remaining water troughs exist, and are kept full, the 392.7 miles between King's Cross and Edinburgh does not by any means represent the limit of non-stop running with No. 4472. Kings Cross to Dundee next time?

A ride on the 'Flying Scotsman'

By Robert J. Herguth

(Taken from Chicago Daily News *July 1970)*

In November 1969 the 'Flying Scotsman' was shipped to the United States. After a hugely successful tour she eventually ended up in San Francisco from where she was eventually shipped back to the UK under new ownership, arriving back in February 1973.

The big British locomotive went "huffa-chuffa-puffa-Chicago-here-we-come."

Its huge green wheels went "clickety-clack, carry-me-back, I-am-the-'Flying-Scotchman'-WHOOMP!"

The gauges on the engine firewall all seemed to read 200 or 40, the firebox glowed yellow-hot, and there was a clear track ahead as we bucked and waltzed on the Norfolk & Western's iron rail road to Chicago.

We were aboard Englishman Alan Pegler's own 'Flying Scotsman' as it merrily hauled a nine-car British train from St. Louis to Dearborn Station for an 11-day stay here.

You realize how ga-ga people still are about steam engines when you're inside the cab of one at 50 miles an hour.

Even at the dustiest Illinois crossroads, mysteriously alerted folks stood and waved and snapped pictures. And showed babes in arms a train they'll remember for life.

Guys hung from the windows of speeding autos, pacing the train on parallel highways, taking home movies of a sight they'll never see again.

Small boys festooned the rails with pennies, to be squashed and cherished forever because they actually touched the 'Flying Scotsman' as it thundered past.

And grizzled 50-year railroad veterans lined up with 3-year-olds to tour the train at the railroad City of Decatur.

And inside the swaying 'Scotsman's' open cab, you realize the truth about speeding coal-burning locomotives.

They are the Ultimate Trip because they touch all five senses.

You taste the smoke from the stack and sniff the cinders, and wherever you hang on, there is the feel of warm and oily iron.

And the 'Scotsman' uncovers the other senses: The sense of pride, and of nostalgia for times past, and of urgency as a great metal beast goes about an urgent endeavor.

Why is Alan Pegler, 50, wealthy English train buff, driving his 'Flying Scotsman', Britain's most famous coal locomotive, across the United States at enormous expense?

"From the monetary point of view, it makes no sense at all," Pegler shouted cheerily between whistle toots.

A young boy studies the huge wheels of the 'Flying Scotsman' on its trip to the United States.

"I'm letting a generation that's growing up see something they won't be able to see.

"And I very much wanted to bring this to America."

Pegler saved the 'Flying Scotsman' from the wrecker by buying it. It gained renown as the first European locomotive to do an authenticated 100 miles an hour. And it was on the crack 393-mile London – Edinburgh nonstop passenger run from 1923 to 1963.

Pegler, who looks a bit like Errol Flynn, brought his locomotive to America by ship last year. It rolled from Boston to Texas, where it wintered, and it is headed toward the National Railway Museum at Green Bay, Wis., and Canada.

The train's nine British rail cars are a rolling museum. One of its Pullmans was used by Ike and Sir Winston Churchill during World War II.

Chicagoans may tour the train – $1 for adults, 50 cents for children – at Dearborn Station from 10 a.m. to 8 p.m. through July 17, and 10 a.m. to 6 p.m. July 18.

Aboard when it arrived at Chicago Tuesday evening were about 25 English and American train buffs, including Davina Flint, ex-British airline employee, and Jim Adams of 1520 Wolfram, president of the Midwest Railway Historical Society.

Pegler's English aide, Pauline Graves, who looks like a young Katherine Hepburn, said it for all train buffs when she peered up at the 'Flying Scotsman' Wednesday here:

"She's lovely, isn't she?"

The train is on a trade mission to the United States and will be shipped back to England in October.

George Hinchcliffe

Railway enthusiast who helped rescue the 'Flying Scotsman' and then built a model rail network in his loft

(Taken from Daily Telegraph *Obituary 4 October 2011)*

George Hinchcliffe, who died on September 20, 2011 aged 89, was one of the great railway modellers of his day and brought home Britain's most famous steam locomotive, No 4472 'Flying Scotsman', from exile in the United States.

A schoolmaster by profession, Hinchcliffe's association with LNER A3 No 4472 'Flying Scotsman' began in 1969, when its then owner, Alan Pegler, took the locomotive to the United States as part of an "exhibition train" in which British companies could promote their exports.

Pegler employed Hinchcliffe first as locomotive manager and then, as it became clear that the tour was becoming a financial disaster, as tour manager. Hinchcliffe rose to the occasion, bringing his considerable skills as a showman to what he called "the circus". In 1970 the train toured the American mid-west and Canada, stopping not only in the big cities but also at small towns, where it proved a big hit with the locals.

The debts already incurred, however, could not be made up, and the locomotive was mothballed in San Francisco. Hinchcliffe returned to Britain, where he became headmaster of a school for Ugandan Asian refugees at RAF Hemswell in Lincolnshire and concentrated on building "O" gauge model trains.

His connection with the locomotive was re-established in 1973 thanks to the enthusiasm of Sir William McAlpine, 6th Bt.

McAlpine later said: "I asked myself, do I want a locomotive in San Francisco? So I said [to Hinchcliffe], if I buy it can you get it back? He reckoned he could."

Hinchcliffe went to San Francisco, negotiated a deal with the outstanding creditors and arranged for 'Flying Scotsman' to be shipped home via the Panama Canal, McAlpine financing the whole operation. In February 1973 the locomotive arrived in Liverpool, then steamed past thousands of people lining the tracks to Derby locomotive works, where it was overhauled.

Hinchcliffe again became manager of 'Flying Scotsman', at its new home at the Steamtown Railway Museum, Carnforth, Lancashire, where he managed both the museum and the carriage works. Steamtown was developed into a centre for restoring locomotives and carriages, its work including the refurbishment of Pullman Cars for the Orient Express.

George Hinchcliffe and the 'Flying Scotsman'.

George Durant Hinchcliffe was born on February 17 1922 at Gainsborough, Lincolnshire, where the LNER railway ran close by his home. He learned to read before starting school by deciphering the nameplates of locomotives; his first job afterwards was as an apprentice steam fitter.

In 1941 he joined the Navy and served in minesweepers for the remainder of the war. Demobbed in 1947, he took a two-year teacher training course at Padfield, near Warrington, then secured a teaching post at Sturton by Stow, near Gainsborough. By the time he left to become manager of 'Flying Scotsman' in 1969 he had risen to become deputy headmaster of the secondary·modern school at Sturton.

During the war Hinchcliffe had met his first wife, Frances Baxter. When they met, he asked how tall she was. She replied: "Four foot eight and a half", and he knew she was the girl for him – that being the Standard Railway Gauge.

Hinchcliffe retired in 1981 and, after Frances's death in 1984, he built an "O" gauge model railway – including a scale model of Glenfinnan Viaduct – in their garden at the village of Hest Bank, near Lancaster.

Hinchcliffe had first become interested in model railways in 1935, and in the late 1940s he co-founded the Gainsborough Model Railway Society. Housed in a converted school, it is reputedly now the third-largest "O" gauge model railway in the world, reproducing traffic on the East Coast main line from Kings Cross to Leeds Central from the late 1930s to the end of the British Railways steam era.

George Hinchcliffe's "O" gauge model layout.

There are 185 locomotives altogether (the first 52 of which were hand-built by Hinchcliffe himself); around 100 coaches; 200 wagons and vans; 150 points; around half a mile of track; and nine stations. The entire system covers 2,500 sq ft and requires 10 operators.

In 1995 he married Janet West, and they moved to the nearby village of Galgate, where Hinchcliffe's "O" gauge layout occupied the entire loft of their house. The railway has 40 locomotives (all built by himself), more than 30 carriages and around 60 wagons. When "playing trains", Hinchcliffe wore a Ffestiniog Railway cap, or sometimes a child's yellow fireman's helmet (to prevent hurting his head on the rafters).

George Hinchcliffe made a cameo appearance as an engine driver in the film of Ronald Harwood's play *The Dresser* (1983). He also wrote a private memoir for this family, *An Obsession with Steam: The Memoirs of George D. Hinchcliffe*.

He is survived by his second wife and by two daughters and a son of his first marriage.

Fortuitous

(Taken from The Railway Magazine *January 2006)*

The country owes Sir William McAlpine and George Hinchcliffe an enormous debt for bringing the 'Flying Scotsman' back to Liverpool from North America in 1973. Once back in good running order, she did some wonderful work based on Carnforth and remained the property of Sir William McAlpine until 1996.

A younger Bill McAlpine with 'Flying Scotsman' at Carnforth in 1976.

Sir William McAlpine (Bill) takes up the story: "I'd met 'Scotsman's' owner, Alan Pegler, at the Ffestiniog Railway a few years earlier but didn't know him very well and, to be honest hadn't been keeping fully up to date with the loco's American travels. So it came as something of a surprise when I went to San Francisco with my wife in 1972 and was told that 'a British engine' was there. I went to Fisherman's Wharf to see it and met the train's tour manager, George Hinchcliffe, who confessed that things weren't going too well.

"Then, back in Britain at the end of that year, I got a call from Alan Bloom, of Bressingham, telling me Alan Pegler had gone bankrupt and would I be interested in joining a rescue syndicate to save 4472.

"I acted quickly ... I suppose you could say I jumped the gun but I knew that putting together a rescue package would cause delay. I paid for George to fly back to the US and find out what was possible. He called me a few days later to say he'd negotiated a purchase price of $72,000 (about £25,000 at the time) but that if I wanted to go ahead, I had to act within the next few hours or it would be too late!

"I said to him, 'Look if I buy it, can you get it back home, otherwise all I've done is buy a big problem! Shipping a loco across the Atlantic wasn't really the sort of thing I wanted to ask the other McAlpine directors to help me with.

"Amazingly, it turned out that George had been sitting next to a shipping manager on the flight over and had been able to arrange for 4472 to be brought home via the Panama Canal.

"I paid off all the outstanding debts owed to the American and Canadian railroads over which Alan's train had run and also picked up the tab for the shipping costs.

The latter alone came to about $35,000, but at least I wasn't going to have 100-odd tons of metal sitting on the other side of the world." (For more on this nail-biting period in 4472's life, see the Alan Pegler Interview in The RM, June '01.)

Once the Pacific had survived the voyage across the Atlantic in January/February 1973, Bill spent a further £11,000 putting it through Derby Works and then ran it on the Torbay Steam Railway for a summer season before taking it to Market Overton to join Pendennis Castle.

Somewhat surprisingly, he revealed to me: "I didn't set out to buy 'Flying Scotsman'... I didn't even have a particular soft spot for A3s! I just knew it was the last of its class and that it would have been a tragedy not to have tried to save it. I owned it for 23 years – only two less than the LNER! – and really grew to love the old girl, yet in all that time I never really thought of her as mine. I always felt she belonged to the nation."

Then, jokingly, he adds: "She was indeed like a beautiful lady – lovely to look at but very expensive to keep."

By 1976, one of Bill's other ladies , had become his sole property and had been moved to Steamtown, the ex-LMS engine sheds at Carnforth, Lancs, on which Bill had then centred much of his main line operation. That year, he was leaving church in his home village one Sunday when he was approached by an agent acting for the Pilbara Railway in Australia, asking if he would sell it to them. "What!", exclaimed Bill. "It would be more than my life's worth!"

The poor fellow looked crestfallen, whereupon the loco owner said: "But you can have !"

That's how No. 4079 came to spend the next 24 years of its life on the other side of the world – the entire cost of buying it and shipping it out in 1977 equating to just 90 minutes' mining output from the Pilbara Society's parent company, Harnersley Iron.

In 1975, Bill had helped set up the Steam Locomotive Operators' Association (SLOA) and for much of the next decade and a half, busied himself primarily on the main line scene, operating Flying Scotsman Enterprises and its marketing and charter arm, Flying Scotsman Services.

Jubilee

The name was synonymous with Carnforth and main line specials – and many thousands of enthusiasts have particularly special memories of 4472's Diamond Jubilee year of 1983. In conjunction with those celebrations, the Pacific hauled passenger trains along the East Coast Main Line on consecutive weekends in early

1983, with guests riding on the open-verandah of one of Bill's wooden saloons at the rear! How times have changed since then.

Away from the BR scene, the UK's leading railfan was also active on the smaller gauges, buying the 2ft 6in gauge Manning Wardle 0-6-2T from Bowaters and forming a company called Pleasure Rail, which specialised in providing clients with 'ready-to-run' narrow gauge systems, complete with tracks, coaches and operating staff. Said Bill. "That all started when Whipsnade Zoo said it wanted a railway to take visitors around its animal paddocks. I already had so I arranged for a 2ft 6in system to be laid down and that became what is now the Great Whipsnade Railway.

The next stage in Bill's life proved to be one of the highest in profile. He agreed to allow 'Flying Scotsman' to be subjected once again to the risks of a long sea voyage – this time to Australia for that nation's bicentennial celebrations of 1988. The Pacific, which had the year before been moved from Carnforth to a new home at Southall, west London, duly left Tilbury docks in September '88 and spent the next 13 months plying its trade 'down under'.

Bill flew out to experience part of the tour and counts his ride on the footplate into Alice Springs in August of 1989 as one of the great highlights of this ownership of the engine.

It was wonderful," he said. "All the schoolchildren had been given the morning off to stand at the lineside and cheer us as we entered the town and it seemed the whole town had turned out to greet us."

During its stay in Australia, the A3 added yet another world record to its extraordinary list of credentials, achieving the longest non-stop run ever for a steam locomotive – 422 miles from Parkes to Broken Hill. And in Perth it met up again with – "something I never thought in my wildest dreams would happen when I sold the 'Castle'," smiled Bill.

Bill inherited the rest of the estate, along with the baronetcy, when his father died in 1990 and he is now officially known as The Hon. Sir William McAlpine Bt., FRSE, FCIT, FRSA.

That same year, an era came to an end when he sold his controlling share in Steamtown Carnforth but, three years later, he began to forge a working partnership with millionaire pop impresario Pete Waterman.

The privatisation of British Rail was about to get underway, affording potentially fabulous opportunities for entrepreneurs, and the two men decided they would be better prepared for the changes ahead if they merged their companies. Out of Flying Scotsman Enterprises and Waterman Railways was thus created a new company, Flying Scotsman Railways, with Sir William and Pete as chairman and vice-chair respectively.

Said Bill at the time: "I am not immortal and if I had died without making plans, 'Flying Scotsman' could possibly have ended up in a situation that would not have been in its best interests."

Under the deal, the men became co-owners of a large fleet of 24 locomotives and 50 carriages (including the ex-'Hull Pullman' Met-Camm set and the BN91 rake of Mk 1s) and to that they added the InterCity Special Trains Unit – the first major operational part of BR to be sold off – in March 1995.

Putting the developments of the early 1990s into historical context, Bill explained: "Back in the early days of SLOA, InterCity's David Ward had complained to us about chartering his coaches but returning them dirty and had suggested us having our own set. So I'd purchased the Met-Camms on the basis that we'd be able to recoup the money within three or four years, which was fine until asbestos was discovered. I thus spent a lot of money having them decontaminated and in the process lost a whole season of income, which set off an overdraft that just carried on growing."

"When I went into business with Pete, the intention was that he would guarantee the overdraft and run the carriages, but for one reason or another things didn't work out and so we agreed to an orderly divorce. We parted amicably, we're still good mates."

Pete took the Crewe-based side of the operation and turned it into the now successful L&NWR company, while Bill retained the Rail Charter Services division. As a result of the amalgamation, 'Flying Scotsman' had also become jointly owned, but its sale to Oxfordshire businessman Dr Tony Marchington for £1.3m in 1996 was handled by Bill. The loco was in pieces in Southall shed at the time with no immediate prospect of being overhauled and, says Bill, "the decision to sell it, along with the coaches, was forced purely by the need to pay off the overdraft."

He recounts with some amusement how Dr Marchington came to his home to discuss the same and did some mental arithmetic "in which he seemed to be allowing for the cost of the taxi waiting outside before deciding whether to buy!"

Steam in the Blood

(*Taken from* Railways in the Blood *by R.H.N. Hardy, 1985*)

A stirring sight is old 4472! The safety valves are buzzing at 215 psi, the fireman has given her a round, smoke of the right sort, the fire blazing white. Driver Jimmy Lister of Carlisle is a happy man, so is his fireman and all's well with the world up the Drag!

Steam in the Blood has never stopped me seeing the way ahead. Events have proved that. We could never again tolerate steam as the prime mover of our network but it still has a magic touch. One would think that enough is enough in retirement but, on the contrary, there is time now and again to thrill once more to the challenge of steam and, provided people don't go mad, the Long Drag is not yet our master although, in the words of Driver Lew Bell of South Lynn, there is a particular necessity 'Always to be ready' these days. The best advice to a fireman, it had been drilled into me from my earliest days on the railway as had the need to avoid smoke and blowing off when so doing.

These lessons served me well in the summer of 1981 when I fired the 'Flying Scotsman', born the same year as me, up the Drag from Appleby. I had been able to make up my own fire in the sidings. There was plenty to bite at, though not as much as one would have had years ago, and one could adjust matters to avoid the smoke and blowing off which can so easily frighten the children. The driver was Jimmy Lister of Carlisle, once of St Margarets, Edinburgh and he knew his 'A3'. Before we started, I asked his advice on whether to push forward the fire from immediately under the firehole door as we departed. He said to leave well alone. I did nothing for the first minute or so by which time Jim had the engine set for a fast acceleration. Immediately, the boiler responded, the first firing produced sufficient smoke to tell me that all was well and the exhaust injector was set to work and was never touched again until we were within less than a mile from the summit. The pressure never strayed from the red mark and the live steam injector could be used to check blowing off and wasting steam. The regulator was wide open from start to finish and all variations to cut off were made gradually so that there was no sudden demand on the boiler and on my back and arms. Between the two of us, we served up the classic recipe for good results. The firehole trapdoor remained open throughout the journey thus cutting down the emission of smoke, and finally and to my delight it was cold and pouring with rain, for the classic recipe means little and often firing and a clean footplate with little time to pause for breath. We climbed to Ais Gill in 29min 38sec, and that was not too bad

'Flying Scotsman' 4472 at Birkett Common on the Settle and Carlisle Railway, 19 August 1981. In the cab is driver Jimmy Lister and firing the engine is R.H.N. Hardy.

for a couple of old gentlemen although it was Jim's handling of the locomotive that set it up for me.

It was an unforgettable journey. George Gordon, our Inspector, had tripped and fallen, breaking his shoulder between Carlisle and Appleby. None of us realised this, nor did George and he maintained a remarkable feat of endurance until he was much nearer home. He had to spend the night in hospital in Carlisle and was off work for several months! I realised, perhaps for the first time, how the fireman occupies the centre of the stage. By arrangement, visitors were allowed to come through the corridor tender to observe what was happening. They came briefly one by one, into an extraordinary world of heat, noise, driving rain, strength and movement. They would see the driver in his corner, with the inspector behind him, the fireman in almost constantly vigorous activity in front of the blinding, white hot fire in the centre of the footplate. As for me, I was oblivious to everything and everybody except the job in hand, to get to Ais Gill in perfect order with a heavy train.

Jimmy Lister and I had never met until he stepped aboard at Appleby. But when, at Garsdale, he turned to me and said: 'Well, Mr Hardy, I'm not sure who you are but you are a credit to your profession', I felt 10ft tall. Here was I, nearly 58 years of age with over 40 years' experience behind me and yet I felt like that. But then steam has the power, the magic touch to do these things.

RIGHT: *Inside the cab of the 'Flying Scotsman' and below is a key to the main instruments and controls.*

1 Regulator handle

2 Reversing screw handle

3 Clutch for reversing gear

4 Air brake handle

5 Straight air brake handle

6 AWS Controller

7 Blower valve

8 Live steam injector steam and delivery valve

9 Live steam injector control wheel

10 Water gauge glass protector

11 Water gauge shut-off cock

12 Water level test cock

13 Exhaust steam injector (H class) control wheel

14 Right Hand injector clack box

15 Exhaust steam injector steam and delivery valve

16 Washout plugs

17 Coal watering pipe (control cock out of sight)

18 Firehole door

19 Trap door (adjustable)

20 Mouthpiece

21 Firedoor lock

22 Fire screens

23 Cut-off indicator (partially hidden)

24 Single gauge for train pipe

25 Duplex gauge for main reservoir and equalling pipe

26 Single gauge for engine brake cylinder pressure

27 Speedometer

28 Steam chest pressure gauge

29 Air brake steam stop valve

30 Blower stop valve

31 Boiler pressure gauge stop valve

32 Carriage heating stop valve

33 Roof ventilator

34 Manifold with shut-off cock hidden which controls supply to 29–32

35 Boiler pressure gauge

36 Regulator stuffing box

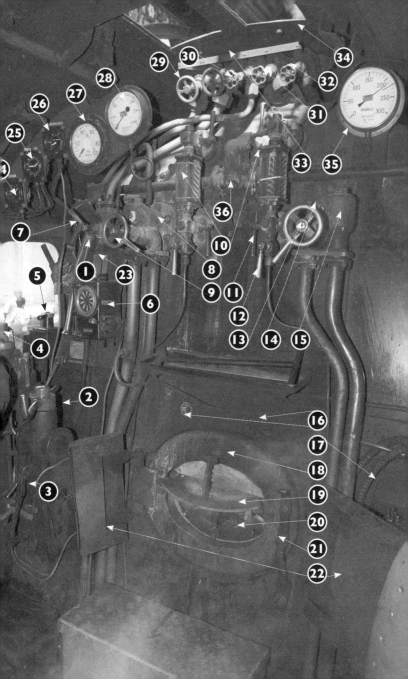

'Flying Scotsman's' Australian Marathon

12,500 MILES UNDER ITS BELT ALREADY – AND 4472 IS GAME FOR MORE

(Taken from The Railway Magazine, *September 1989)*

Flashback to October 16 last year, as 'Flying Scotsman's' tender is lifted by a floating crane in Sydney Harbour.

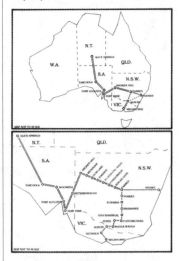

The route of what was intended to be 'Flying Scotsman's' last incredible journey across the Island Continent to Alice Springs – but now there might be more to come with a final railtour to Perth and Western Australia.

It's been one of the greatest steam locomotive journeys of all time; one that those lucky enough to have witnessed will be talking about for many years to come – yet amazingly, the travels of A3 Pacific No. 4472 'Flying Scotsman' Down Under are far from over yet.

Even though the A3 had already put 12,500 miles under its wheels in revenue-earning service at the other side of the world by the end of June, seeing more of Australia than most Australians, it is currently in the middle of a marathon journey to the baking 'Red Heart' of the island continent at Alice Springs, and there's now the distinct possibility of yet another extended stay which may take 'Flying Scotsman' to Perth and Western Australia.

The long tour to Alice Springs was due to begin in spectacular fashion on Sunday, August 6 when No. 4472 left Melbourne accompanied by Australian locomotive No. R761. At Somerton, another Australian loco, No. R707, was waiting to take part in the first three-train 'parallel run' to Seymour, where R707 departed. R761 was to continue parallel to 'Flying Scotsman' all the way to the border town of Albury-Wodonga.

Few Australian settings could exude such a 'British' flavour as this one, as 'Flying Scotsman' and locomotive 5910 steam on to the Picton Viaduct in New South Wales.

After being serviced, No. 4472 was due to leave for an overnight stay in Wagga-Wagga.

On Monday, August 7, 'Flying Scotsman' was to steam through the wheatfields and sheep-farming country of mid-western New South Wales, arriving in Parkes in the late afternoon.

Next day, a journey to the 'silver city' of Broken Hill was on the agenda, and No. 4472's passengers briefly explored the mining town before a mid-morning departure on Wednesday, August 9 for Peterborough, South Australia.

More exotic countryside was on the schedule for 'Flying Scotsman' the following day, when it was due to steam through the hills towards Port Pirie on the shores of the Spencer Gulf.

After a short break, No. 4472 was due to reach Port Augusta for a two-day stopover, allowing Roland Kennington, Dave Rollins and crew to prepare the apple green Pacific for its nail-biting journey across the desert to Alice Springs, and unheard-of temperatures.

Hopefully, Sunday, August 13 would prove a lucky day for 'Flying Scotsman' as it travelled where no steam locomotive had travelled before. After an evening service stop in the desert at Tarcoola, the train was to carry on into the night towards Alice Springs, and an unforgettable sunrise reflecting in the A3's boiler casing.

The train was due to arrive at Alice in the searing heat of lunchtime, before taking a well-deserved five-day stop-

The 'Flying Scotsman' arriving at Alice Springs in Ausut 1989. This was a memorable occasion as the old narrow gauge line had just been replaced with standard guage and she was the first steam locomotive in Alice Springs for many years.

over while its passengers went off to explore the area around Ayer's Rock.

On Saturday, August 19, it is planned that No. 4472 will take part in a short parallel run with the recently restored 'Old Ghan'.

Next day, the A3 leaves Alice at midnight, enabling passengers to take in the landscape which was hidden in the darkness on the outward run. The scheduled arrival at Port Augusta is on Tuesday, August 22.

The rest of the journey to Sydney will be via Adelaide (for a long stopover) on August 23, Peterborough on August 28, Broken Hill on August 29, Parkes on August 30, a day run to Orange and Bathurst on August 31, and arrival back in Sydney, on Friday, September 1, for what was to have been a farewell dinner before No. 4472 began preparations for its sea voyage home to Britain.

However, in the last few weeks another development came up and Flying Scotsman Services Ltd. is to negotiate for yet another extension.

A commercial organisation has intimated that it will put up the money for No. 4472 to visit Perth and Western Australia, and Bernard Staite of FSS was preparing to leave Britain on August 8 to take part in the negotiations.

Perth is the last big Australian capital for 'Flying Scotsman' to conquer; the last big trip across that vast wasteland

FLYING SCOTSMAN

Melbourne 9th July — 6th August P&O Containers

A Poster featuring the 'Flying Scotsman', which was able to operate out of Melbourne. Because there were two standard gauge lines and one 3ft-6in line in parallel, organisers were able to arrange for three steam-hauled trains to run side by side which attracted thousands of onlookers.

before a possible departure back to Britain at the end of October.

The much travelled locomotive should reach Tilbury, and ultimately Southall, just before Christmas.

Before the epic journey to Australia's 'Red Heart' began, No. 4472 had not failed once on the road, a glowing testimony to the caring skills of Roland Kennington, of Bradford, and Dave Rollins, of London, who have been nursing the A3 since last October.

Roland and Dave have been overwhelmed by the Australians' hospitality and enthusiasm for 'Flying Scotsman' and have been quite unable to take up all the invitations they have received during their stay.

After a fairly easy winter at home, which will give Roland and Dave plenty of time to recoup and tell and re-tell their adventures Down Under, 'Flying Scotsman' will probably return to the British main lines in April.

4472: THE PEOPLE'S ENGINE AT LAST!

National Railway Museum buys the 'Flying Scotsman' for £2.2million after campaign raises a staggering

£3.1m

(Taken from The Railway Magazine *June 2004)*

By THE EDITOR

One of the most extraordinary episodes in British railway history has ended with the most famous locomotive in the world being saved for the nation.

The 'Flying Scotsman' will now take a richly-deserved place in the National Collection alongside the other great masterpieces of the railway world.

Forty one years after being sold into private hands by the State for £3,000, it has made the return journey as part of a campaign worth no less than a thousand times that amount!

For £3.1million is the breathtaking sum raised by the public and institutions of Great Britain to ensure that this icon of British engineering remained in the country of its origin and among the people who have taken it to heart.

Of that huge amount, the actual sale price amounts to £2.2m – a high price but one the Head of the National Railway Museum, Andrew Scott, was prepared to pay to ensure that the sole-surviving Gresley A3 Pacific was not lost abroad or sold into another period of uncertainty in the hands of a private individual.

The gripping story of how he and his team succeeded is told exclusively through the pages of his personal diary in this issue of *The Railway Magazine*. It reveals his innermost fears and concerns as the clock ticked down to the deadline by which sealed bids had to be submitted. It reveals how his museum team pulled together to ensure their quarry did not escape – and it reveals how the National Heritage Memorial Fund and billionaire Sir Richard Branson entered the arena to enable the museum to clinch the deal of a lifetime.

It is a story of true British grit and resolve worthy of 'Flying Scotsman' itself.

As has been reported at length in the April and May issues of *The Railway Magazine*, No. 4472 was put up for sale by Flying Scotsman plc in mid-February. The company had taken the reluctant decision to dispose of its major asset in order to recuperate debts of £1.5m racked up in an ill-conceived venture to market the ex-L.N.E.R. Pacific through a proposed visitor centre near Edinburgh Waverley.

It was simply the latest in a long line of financial misfortune that seems to have dogged the private owners of the locomotive since it was bought by Retford businessman Alan Pegler back in 1963. Alan, now 84, has been keeping a close watch on the proceedings and is absolutely delighted at the outcome (see foot of this page) see over.

Also delighted is Stephen Johnson, Head of the National Heritage Memorial Fund, whose organisation did most to make the purchase possible by contributing the lion's share of the price – no less than £1.8m in fact.

In a telling quote which puts 'Scotsman's' true importance in the national psyche into perspective, he said: "What could possibly be a better use of our money than to save such a magnificent piece of British engineering?"

LEGENDARY

The £900,000 balance of funds the NRM has left over after payment of the purchase price, buyer's premium and other miscellaneous costs, will, says Mr Scott, form a fighting fund from which the locomotive's next heavy overhaul will be funded in two years. "This will help to ensure that the engine stays on the main line, where it belongs," he says.

In between duties, No. 4472 will be displayed at either York or the NRM's new outstation at Shildon. When in York, it will reside in a special display and interpretation zone created by Yorkshire Forward, a regional development agency that stepped into the fray with a grant of half a million pounds purely for that purpose!

The timing of the purchase is perfect where the NRM's bicentenary Railfest is concerned, for the near-legendary Pacific will now be the centrepiece of that extravaganza. Once a hotbox, incurred on the engine's last run on January 10, has been repaired at its current home depot of Southall, west London, it is hoped to use the loco to haul a Railfest launch special along old Yorkshire stamping grounds from Doncaster to York to formally open the festival at the end of May.

The only people who don't appear to have come out of the deal well (although most will be overjoyed regardless) are the shareholders of FS plc. Not only were they not even afforded the courtesy of a letter at any stage of the sale proceedings but there is no guarantee of how much, if anything, will be left over to disperse among them.

Said one: "The company has acted shoddily over this and seems to have taken advantage of the fact that most of us bought our shares not as investments but for reasons of enthusiasm. At least we know the loco now safely belongs to us all anyway!"

Another man uncertain of his long term future is the locomotive's chief engineer, Roland Kennington. A first class exponent of his trade, Roland knows every nut and bolt of 4472 and, with only a tiny team of helpers, has kept the machine in working order, against often daunting odds, for many years. It is understood he will be staying with the new owners, even if only during the transition period.

New ownership brings new opportunities, and among those mooted are a return to BR Brunswick green livery (which apart from a test run has never been seen on the main line in preservation), a return to single chimney form and maybe even early BR blue livery.

Whatever, the future is exciting.

Branson: A personal thankyou to *The Railway Magazine* and its readers

Sir Richard Branson attended the official announcement of the sale at Southall and after spraying the locomotive with champagne told RM editor Nick Pigott: "Chris Green at Virgin Trains drew my attention to the appeal in your magazine and I realised I had to try to get involved in saving the loco. Your readers have been magnificent. Please thank them all."

Worth the wait! Pegler and McAlpine get their wishes

The sale of 'Flying Scotsman' to the NRM rights a serious wrong perpetrated back in the early 1960s when the authorities of the day decreed that Gresley non-streamlined Pacifics had insufficient claim to be worthy of official preservation in the National Collection.

That was despite them being Britain's oldest surviving Pacific design and despite the fact that No. 4472 was the first British engine to officially break the 100mph barrier.

Alan Pegler, who spent his own money rectifying that situation, told *The Railway Magazine*: "I have waited over 40 years for this. I am a very happy man today."

The sale will also strike a chord for the loco's second private owner, Sir William McAlpine, who said in the March 1996 edition of *The Railway Magazine*: "Scotsman is special to millions of people. My dearest wish would be to see it owned by the public."

THE DONORS

(All totals approximate)

NHMF:	£1,800,000
Yorkshire Forward:	£500,000
Sir Richard Branson:	£365,000

Sir Richard Branson on the footplate of the 'Flying Scotsman' at the opening of the National Railway Museum's Railfest 2004.

Members of the public:	£287,000
The Railway Magazine readers:	£50,000
Alan Moore:	£50,000
Leo de Rothschild:	£25,000
Friends of the NRM:	£20,000
The Gresley Society:	£2,000
NELPG:	£1,000

THE BIDDERS

(Total seven. Four anon, inc one from abroad)

National Railway Museum:	£2.2m
Moiz Saigara:	£2.1m
Jeremy Hosking:	unknown
Anon:	£600,000
(Agent's commission	£110,000)

The 'Flying Scotsman' – the future

The 'Flying Scotsman' pictured in the NRM's Works on 19 June following Railfest 2012.

After appearing at the NRM's Railfest 2012 (June 2–10) A3 No. 4472 'Flying Scotsman' entered the York's Museum Works where the pipework, valve gear and lubrication sysetem received attention. However, it was soon noted that more work was required and the National Railway Museum commissioned two reports. The first was written by Bob Meanley, chief engineer at Tyseley Locomotive Works and assisted by Professor Roger Kemp, Professor of Engineering at Lancaster University. This report looked at the overall problems the NRM has had since it owned the engine and the long delay in getting the locomotive back into working order. The second report was produced by First Class Partnerships and looks at the proposed programme of works required to restore the locomotive.

There are number of major problems associated with the boiler, cylinders and firebox and the NRM, at time of publication, had invited tenders from outside contractors to undertake much of this work.

Another recommendation in the reports was that an annual mileage limit of 6,500 to 7,000 miles should be imposed with each train between 250 and 350 miles. This would allow around 25 main line trips a year satisfying demand and conserving the engine for maximum long-term use in terms of wear and tear.

The hope is that 'Flying Scotsman' will be back in operation sometime in 2014.